PRO BASKETBALL
Its Superstars and History

PRO BASKETBALL
Its Superstars and History

Edited by Zander Hollander

An Associated Features Book

SBS SCHOLASTIC BOOK SERVICES
New York Toronto London Auckland Sydney

COVER PHOTO: **George Kalinsky**

Some of the material in this book appears in THE MODERN ENCYCLOPEDIA OF BASKETBALL, a hardcover book published by Four Winds Press, a division of Scholastic, and is available through your local bookstore or directly from Four Winds Press, 50 West 44 Street, New York, N. Y. 10036.

1st printing ....January 1971

Printed in the U.S.A.

CONTENTS

Introduction..8
I THE GREATEST PROS.......................................10

  1 LEW ALCINDOR: A New Era 11
  2 PAUL ARIZIN: Line-Drive Jumper 16
  3 RICK BARRY: On and Off Court 19
  4 ELGIN BAYLOR: Twisting All-Star 22
  5 CARL BRAUN: Two-Hand Over-Head 25
  6 WILT CHAMBERLAIN: Record Collector 28
  7 BOB COUSY: Houdini of the Hardwood 32
  8 JOE FULKS: Link to the Moderns 36
  9 NEIL JOHNSTON: Master of the Hook 39
 10 ED MACAULEY: The Skinny Center 42
 11 GEORGE MIKAN: Mr. 99 45
 12 VERN MIKKELSEN: Big Guy from Hamline 48
 13 BOB PETTIT: Head of the Class 51
 14 JIM POLLARD: Corner Man 54
 15 FRANK RAMSEY: Supersub 57
 16 OSCAR ROBERTSON: Big O 60
 17 BILL RUSSELL: Noble Defender 63
 18 DOLPH SCHAYES: Iron Man 67
 19 BILL SHARMAN: Robot Shooter 70
 20 JACK TWYMAN: More than a Player 74
 21 JERRY WEST: The Eternal Quest 77

II MODERN PRO HISTORY 80
   NBA Yearly Roundups, Standings,
   Playoff Results, Individual Leaders 81

III ALL-TIME NBA TEAMS AND RECORDS 178

PRO BASKETBALL
Its Superstars and History

INTRODUCTION

As professional basketball entered a new era at the start of the 1970's — the Age of Alcindor — horizons seemed unlimited for the giant responsible, Milwaukee's Lew Alcindor, and for fans of all ages who will be witness to his exploits over the next decade or so.

There was no doubt that the seven-foot-plus product of the playgrounds of New York would add dramatic new dimensions to the game and that big Lew would take his place alongside — and in many instances above — his fellow superstars, and those of yesteryear as well.

Superstars? After his first year in the National Basketball Association, Alcindor was chosen by Joe Lapchick for inclusion among the 21 greatest professionals since World War II. With a half-century in the game — as a player with the Original Celtics, as a college coach, and as coach of the New York Knickerbockers — Lapchick was regarded as one of the keenest observers of basketball talent. The profiles of his 21 selections make up the first section of this book, and these stars come back again in the year-by-year history and records that comprise the second half of the book.

The goal here was two-fold: to tell the tale of the superstars, and to document the facts and figures of the National Basketball Association, which began its 25th year with the 1970–71 campaign.

Some of the material in the book first appeared in *The Modern Encyclopedia of Basketball*, published by Four Winds Press, a division of Scholastic, Inc.

The editor wishes to acknowledge the contributions of writers Sandy Padwe of the Philadelphia *Inquirer* and David Rosen, and the cooperation of Walter Kennedy, commissioner of the National Basketball Association, and Nick Curran, NBA publicist.

Baldwin, New York   Zander Hollander

Joe Lapchick was connected with the game of basketball for more than 50 years. As a player with the original Celtics and many other early teams, as a professional coach with the New York Knickerbockers and a college coach at St. John's University, Lapchick was such a distinguished figure that he inevitably was elected to the Basketball Hall of Fame.

His career stretched from the early days of the modern era. Lapchick had seen virtually every outstanding player and all the great teams. Naturally, choosing the top players must be a subjective process. One can not measure greatness on statistics alone. Many intangibles — ranging from desire to often unsung skills such as defense and playmaking — serve as a truer yardstick than scoring average.

Lapchick took all this into account when he chose the following as the 21 greatest pros of the modern (post World War II) era.

THE GREATEST PROS

Nobody, including New York's championship Knicks, could fault selection of Milwaukee's Lew Alcindor as NBA Rookie of the Year.

VERNON BIEVER

Since that day in 1891 when Dr. James Naismith invented the game, basketball has never seen a big man like Lew Alcindor. Bill Russell may have been a more intimidating defensive figure; Wilt Chamberlain at his best was stronger and scored more points, and Willis Reed has a better outside shot. But none of basketball's giant pivotmen has ever done as many things as well as Big Lew.

In high school, college and in his first pro season with the NBA's Milwaukee Bucks, Alcindor has scored points, grabbed rebounds, blocked shots and handled the ball like no big man before him. Opposing players and coaches have used every conceivable tactic — from attempted physical assault to special collapsing defenses — in futile efforts to neutralize him. In the end, they have all come to the same conclusion: Alcindor just can't be stopped. Sometimes he can be held in check, and on rare occasions he may beat himself with a mistake. But otherwise, he dominates every game in which he plays.

From the time he entered Power Memorial Academy in New York City as a 6-8 freshman until he graduated from UCLA as a polished 7-1⅜ All-American, every team Alcindor played on won its championship. The Power Panthers ran up a winning streak of 71 consecutive games and won three city Catholic league championships. The UCLA Bruins lost only twice in his three varsity seasons and captured an unprecedented three NCAA championships in succession. As a rookie pro, he led the Bucks, dismal last-place finishers the year before, into the semifinal round of the playoffs before they were eliminated by the New York Knickerbockers.

But somehow these prodigious feats seem only natural for someone of Lew's awesome physical proportions. Ferdinand Lewis Alcindor, Jr., was born large. Nearly two feet tall at birth, and weighing 12 pounds, 11 ounces, he was the only child of a 6-2 subway policeman and a 6-foot housewife. By the time he started school, he already towered more than a foot above his classmates.

On the first day of school, his teacher, seeing him in the back of the room, called out, "You there, please sit down."

Lew answered in a quiet voice, "But I am sitting down."

By the time he was ten years old, Lew already stood more than six feet tall. But like so many other very tall youngsters, his body had grown faster than his coordination. Farrell Hopkins, the coach at St. Jude's, Lew's grammar school in Manhattan, automatically put Lew on the basketball team because of his height. In addition, he set up a program of weight-lifting, rope-jumping, and tennis to increase his strength and coordination. The program obviously worked.

At 13, Lew was 6-8 and weighed 200 pounds. John Donohue, the basketball coach at Power Memorial, heard about Lew and set up a scholarship at Power. New York has always been the home of some of the greatest basketball players, but even by the high New York City standards, Lew's high school career was amazing. In his three high school years, 1962–65, Lew scored 2,067 points and snared 2,002 rebounds, both New York schoolboy records. With Alcindor an irresistible force on offense and an immovable object on defense, the Panthers trounced everyone they faced before finally bowing, 46–43, to powerful DeMatha High of Hyattsville, Maryland.

College coaches across the nation quickly realized that having Alcindor on the team would turn any school into a national basketball power. Scholarship offers soon poured in from virtually every college in the land. Coach Donohue screened all the offers and managed to keep the coaches, recruiters, and press away from his superstar. Finally Lew narrowed his choices to UCLA, Michigan, and two local schools, St. John's and New York University. Then he announced at a crowded press conference that he had decided to attend UCLA.

In his first scrimmage as a freshman, Lew scored 30 points against the Bruin varsity. As a sophomore he scored 56 points in his first game for a school scoring record. "I don't care about points," he insisted. "I care about winning. I don't want them to remember me for scoring records." If victories were what he wanted, Lew wasn't disappointed. During his initial varsity season, 1966–67, the Bruins were undefeated national champions. In his junior year they extended the victory streak to 45 games before disaster struck. Battling for a rebound, Lew suffered an eye injury and had to sit out two games.

He returned to action against Houston, the number two team in the country, but he was still suffering from double vision. Before more than 52,000 fans in the Houston Astrodome, Houston's Elvin Hayes scored 39 points to 18 for the handicapped Alcindor, and the unbeaten string was broken at 47. The Bruins began another streak the next game and didn't lose again that year as they won their second consecutive national championship. They gained some revenge, too, by routing Hayes and his Houston teammates in the NCAA semifinals.

Lew's third varsity season looked like a rerun of the first two. The Bruins again lost only one game and won the NCAA title for the third year in a row. Also for the third straight time Alcindor was named the Most Valuable Player in the NCAA tournament. During his three seasons at UCLA, Lew averaged 26.4 points a game and made 62.4 percent of his shots, an NCAA record, as the Bruins won 88 of 90 games. There is no telling how many points he might have scored if coach John Wooden had not stressed a balanced offense and team play.

Following his final college season, Alcindor was drafted by the Milwaukee Bucks of the NBA and the New York Nets of the rival American Basketball Association. Lew asked each team to make only one offer, weighed the two and decided to sign with the Bucks for an estimated $1.4 million.

Lew lost no time in proving that he would be just as powerful a force in the pros as he had been in high school and college. He finished second to the Lakers'

Jerry West in the scoring race with a 28.8 average, and third in rebounding with 14.5 a game. Handling the basketball more like a baseball, Lew topped the league's centers in assists, as he constantly hit the open man with passes. At the close of the season, he won unanimous selection as Rookie of the Year. More important, the Bucks who had won only 27 games the year before, improved to 56 victories, and finished second in the East.

Those who had watched Lew since his high school days in New York were conscious of subtle changes in his play. "I'd like to think I've improved in every way," Lew said after his rookie season. "As for my hook shot, I didn't have to use it much in college. Now I hook more because they're forcing me farther away from the basket." Released from above the rim and virtually unblockable, Lew's hook is truly an awesome sight. But it's not his only offensive weapon. Moving with an effortless fluidity never before seen in a man so big, Lew relies on a variety of hooks, short jumpers, drives, and stuffs for his points.

With many more years of professional basketball ahead of him, and with his skills improving with each game, Alcindor seems a sure bet to dominate the NBA. To many observers, 1969–70, his rookie season, was clearly a prelude to future greatness, the dawning of the Age of Alcindor.

ALCINDOR, FERDINAND LEWIS (Lew)
b. Apr. 16, 1947   Ht. 7-1⅜   Wt. 230
College — UCLA

YR.	TEAM	G	FG	FT	TP	AVG.
1969–70	Miwaukee	82	938	485	2361	28.8

UPI

16

It was like a Renoir or a Rembrandt. Paul Arizin's jump shot was perfection. The best description was this one in a Philadelphia newspaper: "... flicking the ball on the crest of his leap like a man riding an invisible surf, this is Arizin's moment of expression."

Arizin played 10 years in the National Basketball Association for the Philadelphia Warriors. During those 10 years, he averaged 22.8 points per game and won scoring championships in 1951–52 with a 25.4 average and in 1956–57 with 25.6.

There is no telling how much a two-year marine hitch hurt Arizin right after he won his first scoring championship. Certainly, it claimed what might have been two of his most productive years, but even though he missed them, he still had a remarkable career.

Arizin came to the Warriors after making All-American at Villanova University. Even in college, the jump shot was his trademark. "The truth is," Arizin said, "that it [the shot] came by accident. I was playing in the Catholic Club League in Philadelphia and our games were on a slick dance floor. When I tried to hook, my feet would go out from under me. So I jumped. The ceiling was low and I had to throw line drives. I just never changed."

It's a good thing he didn't. The 6-4, 210-pounder played forward for the Warriors and the jump shot enabled him to get the ball away despite defensive counterparts who stood 6-7 and 6-8. Theoretically, big, agile professionals should have been able to stop Arizin. But he possessed marvelous timing and an important intangible called anticipation. Of course, he had natural spring in his legs, but it was the timing and anticipation which often meant the difference between scoring and not scoring.

Arizin was the fifth man in NBA history to reach the 10,000-point mark, and his career high in a single

Paul Arizin is en route to one of his leaping shots.

game was 44 points. At times one wondered how Arizin even made it up and down the court because he was constantly wheezing and seemingly trying to regain his breath. Arizin laughed when people suggested he was not in shape. "That panting and coughing is a sinus condition I've always had. It doesn't hurt my endurance," he said.

And so he would run down the court, gulping for air, an unruly cowlick on the back of his head flopping up and down. He would head for the corner, take a pass, then fake and jump, hanging in the air for a split second before firing his line-drive shot. A second later the ball would nestle in the basket.

ARIZIN, PAUL
b. Apr. 9, 1928   Ht. 6-4   Wt. 200
College — Villanova

YR.	TEAM	G	FG	FT	TP	AVG.
1950–51	Philadelphia	65	352	417	1121	17.2
1951–52	Philadelphia	66	548	578	1674	25.4
1954–55	Philadelphia	72	529	454	1512	21.0
1955–56	Philadelphia	72	617	507	1741	24.2
1956–57	Philadelphia	71	613	591	1817	25.6
1957–58	Philadelphia	68	483	440	1406	20.7
1958–59	Philadelphia	70	632	587	1851	26.4
1959–60	Philadelphia	72	593	420	1606	22.3
1960–61	Philadelphia	79	650	532	1832	23.2
1961–62	Philadelphia	78	611	484	1706	21.9
	Totals	713	5628	5010	16266	22.8

Rick Barry rose fast in the pros.

MALCOLM EMMONS

For seven straight years, Wilt Chamberlain dominated the NBA scoring statistics. Then during the 1965–66 season a rookie named Rick Barry appeared in a San Francisco uniform. That year, Wilt won the scoring championship again. It wasn't until the following season that Rick Barry stunned the basketball world by taking the title from Chamberlain.

Only in his second year, Barry was magnificent, leading the Warriors into the championship finals against the Philadelphia 76ers. As a second-year man, Barry scored 2,775 points in 78 games for a 35.6 points per game average. "In his second year as a pro," said Los Angeles coach Fred Schaus, "he's ahead of Bob Pettit at the same stage. Rick's a better shooter and a little quicker than Bob."

Schaus made the comparison with Pettit because when Rick first entered the league after starring at the University of Miami (Fla.), he was a rather skinny 6-7, 200 pounds. Just like Pettit who went on to become one of the game's greats. And, like Pettit, a lot of people doubted if Barry had the physical assets to take the punishment in the NBA. They found out quickly. As a rookie, he scored 2,059 points for a 25.7 average and he grabbed 850 rebounds. For that performance he was named Rookie of the Year.

During college, Barry, a native of Roselle Park, N.J., was a controversial basketball player. He had a quick temper that often got him into trouble on the court. When he turned professional, he remained just as controversial. That first year was a tough one. Barry took much punishment. The second year wasn't quite as bad. By then, he was recognized as one of the game's superstars. His game improved, too. Not just in scoring, but playmaking also. "He and Elgin Baylor are the greatest passing forwards in the game," San Francisco coach Bill Sharman said. Center Nate Thurmond also praised Barry: "Nobody on the team got the ball into me better than Rick."

Since 1967, Barry's career has been marked as much by legal skirmishes and injuries as by what he has done on the basketball court. After the 1966–67 season he signed a contract with the Oakland Oaks of the newly formed American Basketball Association. Bruce Hale, Barry's father-in-law (and college coach) was the general manager of the Oaks. The Warriors contested the contract with the Oaks in court and Barry was forced to sit out the 1967–68 season as a result.

He finally appeared in an Oakland uniform the following season, but a series of knee injuries limited his playing time to just 35 games. Nevertheless he averaged 34.0 points a game and the Oaks won the ABA title.

In the summer of 1969, the Oaks moved to Washington, D.C., and became the Washington Capitols. Barry wanted to remain in the San Francisco area and tried to jump back to the Warriors. This time the Caps went to court and obtained an injunction forcing Barry to play for the ABA club. Again hampered by knee trouble, Barry played in 52 games, averaging 27.7 points a game. But throughout the season he insisted that he really wanted to play for the Warriors.

BARRY, RICHARD (Rick)
b. Mar. 28, 1944   Ht. 6-7   Wt. 205
College — Miami (Fla.)

YR.	TEAM	G	FG	FT	TP	AVG.
1965–66	San Francisco	80	745	569	2059	25.7
1966–67	San Francisco	78	1011	753	2775	35.6
	NBA Totals	158	1756	1322	4834	30.6
1967–68	Did not play					
1968–69	Oakland ABA	35	392	403	1190	34.0
1969–70	Washington ABA	52	517	400	1442	27.7
	ABA Totals	87	*909	803	2632	30.3

*Includes 11 three-point field goals

MALCOLM EMMONS

It was during a playoff game against the Baltimore Bullets in 1965. Elgin Baylor took a nasty spill. His teammates had to help him from the floor as 16,000 fans in the Los Angeles Sports Arena looked on in stunned silence. Nobody knew it then, but Elgin Baylor had just ripped off part of his kneecap.

The next year was the toughest of Baylor's career. The old, graceful moves didn't seem to be there any more. No more of those twisting driving layups, those unbelievable jump shots. Around the league, they were saying Elgin Baylor — the greatest forward for his size — was through.

For seven years, the 6-5 Seattle graduate had been one of the leading scorers in the league and together with guard Jerry West gave the Lakers the greatest one-two scoring punch ever seen in professional basketball. Despite the pain and the problems brought on by calcium deposits in his knees, Baylor continued to work to strengthen his weak legs. And finally on February 2, 1966, he scored 29 points and grabbed 21 rebounds in a game against Cincinnati. The obituary notices were discarded.

Despite the decreased mobility brought about by his chronic knee problems, Baylor has averaged between 26.6 and 24.0 points a game in the four seasons since his injury.

Baylor is the all-time leading scorer for the Lakers and he ranks second in the league overall. Two years after his injury, he was the most tireless player on the Laker squad, totaling an amazing 3,029 minutes in 77 games, almost 600 more than the number two man on the same team.

Baylor has proven his incredible versatility by leading the Lakers for at least one season each in scoring, rebounding, assists, field goal accuracy, free throw accuracy, and minutes played.

His best scoring year came in 1961–62 when he averaged 38.2 in 48 games. Baylor will be remembered for his sure touch with the ball. At times one

Elgin Baylor does it all in the air.

23

wondered how he cleared opposition defenses. The answer was a combination of agility and muscle. This agility and tremendous spring and strength enabled him to out-rebound forwards much bigger than he was.

When Baylor signed with the Lakers out of Seattle University, he actually saved a faltering franchise. At the time, the Lakers were still playing in Minneapolis. "If he had turned me down then," Laker President Bob Short said at the time, "I'd have been out of business. The club would have gone bankrupt."

Well, Baylor did sign and the Lakers slowly began to regain their old form. However, the team moved to Los Angeles and Baylor became one of the biggest stars in a town which had its share. His presence turned the Lakers' franchise into one of the most rewarding in sports.

He was all-pro first team on ten different occasions and played in eleven All-Star games. In a game against New York in 1960 he scored 71 points. And in a game against Boston in 1959, he scored 64 points. The 71 points stood as a league record until Wilt Chamberlain broke it in 1962.

BAYLOR, ELGIN
b. Sept. 16, 1934   Ht. 6-5   Wt. 225
College — Seattle

YR.	TEAM	G	FG	FT	TP	AVG.
1958–59	Minneapolis	70	605	532	1742	24.9
1959–60	Minneapolis	70	755	564	2074	29.6
1960–61	Los Angeles	73	931	676	2538	34.8
1961–62	Los Angeles	48	680	476	1836	38.2
1962–63	Los Angeles	80	1029	661	2719	34.0
1963–64	Los Angeles	78	756	471	1983	25.4
1964–65	Los Angeles	74	763	483	2009	27.1
1965–66	Los Angeles	65	415	249	1079	16.6
1966–67	Los Angeles	70	711	440	1862	26.6
1967–68	Los Angeles	77	757	488	2002	26.0
1968–69	Los Angeles	76	730	421	1881	24.8
1969–70	Los Angeles	54	511	276	1298	24.0
Totals		835	8643	5737	23023	27.6

5. CARL BRAUN: Two-Hand Over-Head

Carl Braun came into the National Basketball Association without a glittering collegiate reputation. A "nonentity" the papers called him. When Carl Braun retired after the 1961-62 season, he left with one of the best records in professional basketball.

Braun always was a great shooter, but his greatest asset was his adaptability. His best scoring year, for example, did not come until he was in his ninth season with the New York Knickerbockers. That season he scored 1,173 points for a 16.5 average, a tribute to his ability to learn and use this knowledge on the basketball court.

When Braun joined the Knicks, he had no jump shot and only a standard two-hand set shot. Bud Palmer, his roommate, taught him the jump shot. Braun needed it, for at 6-5 he was meeting some stiff defensive opposition when he played forward.

Later, Braun was converted to a backcourt man. Again, he had to adapt. This time, he developed the shot that became his trademark, a two-hand, over-the-head set. The success of this unorthodox shot depended on speed, and for years Braun practiced by bouncing a ball off the wall in a gymnasium and shooting as soon as the ball reached his hands. "As you get older," he said, "you have to play more with your head."

That is exactly what kept Braun around the NBA for 13 years. During those seasons, Braun played in 789 games and scored 10,625 points for a lifetime average of 13.5. He often was the Knicks' leading scorer, their best foul shooter and twice wound up as their leading playmaker.

New York, of course, was long the showcase city of the NBA and the games in Madison Square Garden drew the largest crowds. One of the main reasons the people flocked there was to watch the smooth-operating Braun take on the "name" stars from around the country. More often than not Braun came out ahead.

Braun was not a sensational type ballplayer. He

was steady and could be counted upon in tough situations. He could score, pass, and rebound when he had to. Later in his career, when he became more of a playmaker than a scorer, people constantly asked him about the sudden change. Braun was simply prolonging his career. "Heck," he said, "I'm a New York City ballplayer and give-and-go is New York City ball. I always knew how to handle it." Carl Braun knew how to handle anything connected with basketball.

BRAUN, CARL
b. Sept. 25, 1927   Ht. 6-5   Wt. 180
College — Colgate

YR.	TEAM	G	FG	FT	TP	AVG.
1947–48	New York	47	276	119	671	14.3
1948–49	New York	57	299	212	810	14.2
1949–50	New York	67	373	285	1031	15.4
1952–53	New York	70	323	331	977	14.0
1953–54	New York	71	354	354	1062	14.8
1954–55	New York	70	400	274	1074	15.1
1955–56	New York	72	396	320	1112	15.4
1956–57	New York	72	378	245	1001	13.9
1957–58	New York	71	426	321	1173	16.5
1958–59	New York	72	287	180	754	10.5
1959–60	New York	54	285	129	699	12.9
1960–61	New York	15	37	11	85	5.7
1961–62	Boston	49	78	20	176	3.6
Totals		789	3912	2801	10625	13.5

6. WILT CHAMBERLAIN: Record Collector

MALCOLM EMMONS

The greatest offensive player in the history of basketball. It is as simple as that. From the moment the 7-1 center entered the National Basketball Association for the 1959–60 season, he was an awesome, powerful figure on offense.

He will be remembered most for his scoring ability, but in the latter years of his career his game changed, and as his proficiency on defense increased (and his proficiency at playmaking) so did the records of the teams he played for.

Chamberlain's best season was 1966–67 when he led the Philadelphia 76ers to a World's Championship. That ended — for a while — all the comments about Chamberlain being a great scorer, but not being very valuable when it came to helping his teams win championships. That tag went as far back as his collegiate days at the University of Kansas.

Chamberlain was one of the most publicized high school basketball players in history. He went from Philadelphia's Overbrook High School to Kansas where he played only two varsity years before dropping out to play for Abe Saperstein's Harlem Globetrotters. He joined the NBA the following season.

In his rookie season with the old Philadelphia Warriors, Chamberlain averaged 37.6 points per game. He increased that the next season to 38.4. But it was in 1961–62 that he was at his best as a scorer, finishing with 4,029 points in 80 games, an average of 50.4 points per game. On March 2, 1962, in a game against the New York Knickerbockers at Hershey, Pa., he scored an incredible 100 points on 36 field goals and 28 foul shots.

Chamberlain led the league in scoring for seven straight years until Rick Barry of San Francisco broke his string in 1966–67. He also led the league five times in rebounding, his highest figure being 2,149 in 1960–61. On November 24, 1960, in a game against the

Wilt Chamberlain: Highest-paid pro.

Boston Celtics, Chamberlain set an NBA record with 55 rebounds.

He also won seven field goal percentage titles and was a constant leader in the minutes played department. And in the latter part of his career, he added to his all-time NBA scoring record every time he stepped on the floor. But despite all his records and all his feats, Chamberlain also will be remembered as one of the most controversial figures in the game. A moody, introspective individual, Chamberlain often missed practice sessions, creating friction not only with his coaches, but among his teammates, too. He needed the practice, too, because he was one of the poorest foul shooters in the history of the game. His lifetime average hovered around the 50 per cent mark. He set a number of records for foul shooting which he would like to forget: most foul tries missed in one game (18); most foul tries missed in a season (528); and most foul tries missed in a playoff game (17). Opposing teams often considered it good strategy to foul Chamberlain rather than allow him to attempt a field goal.

Chamberlain, however, established some fantastic individual shooting records. At one point in the 1966–67 season he made 35 straight shots from the field. And he also finished that season with a 68.3 shooting percentage, another record.

A perennial all-league and All-Star team selection, Chamberlain was named the league's Most Valuable Player four times. His place in basketball history can not be disputed. He was considered such a valuable property that he was paid $250,000 for the 1967–68 season by the 76ers.

Before the start of the 1968–69 season, Chamberlain was traded to the Los Angeles Lakers for three players. The 76ers had been unable to reach salary terms with Chamberlain, but Jack Kent Cooke, owner of the Lakers, agreed to pay Chamberlain a reported $3,000,000 for five seasons. This contract made Chamberlain the highest-paid professional athlete in history.

Early in the 1969–70 season Chamberlain suffered a severe knee injury that required surgery and the doctors said that he could forget about playing for the rest of the year. But Wilt insisted he would be back, worked hard on his rehabilitation program and returned late in the campaign to help lead the Lakers into the playoff finals against the New York Knickerbockers.

CHAMBERLAIN, WILT
b. Aug. 21, 1936   Ht. 7-1   Wt. 275
College — Kansas

YR.	TEAM	G	FG	FT	TP	AVG.
1959–60	Philadelphia	72	1065	577	2707	37.6
1960–61	Philadelphia	79	1251	531	3033	38.4
1961–62	Philadelphia	80	1597	835	4029	50.4
1962–63	San Francisco	80	1463	660	3586	44.8
1963–64	San Francisco	70	1204	540	2948	36.9
1964–65	S.F.-Philadelphia	73	1063	408	2534	34.7
1965–66	Philadelphia	79	1074	501	2649	33.5
1966–67	Philadelphia	81	785	386	1956	24.1
1967–68	Philadelphia	82	819	354	1992	24.3
1968–69	Los Angeles	81	641	382	1664	20.5
1969–70	Los Angeles	12	129	70	328	27.3
	Totals	799	11091	5244	27426	34.3

7. BOB COUSY: Houdini of the Hardwood

UPI

It was Joe Fulks and George Mikan who first focused the public's attention on modern-day professional basketball. It was Bob Cousy, however, who made the game fun and attracted the crowds.

Cousy was the best ballhandler and backcourtman in the history of basketball. Writers all over the country constantly thought up new nicknames for him. "The Mobile Magician" was one; "The Houdini of the Hardwood" another. Though the nicknames may have been a little corny, they were accurate. His forte was playmaking, though he was an excellent scorer, too. Cousy's playmaking abilities were due to superb reflexes, a fine knowledge of the game, and peripheral vision which enabled him to command a 180-degree range of the action on the court.

For eight consecutive years (1953–1960), Cousy led the NBA in assists. "Cousy," said Red Auerbach, who coached him in Boston, "was one of the greatest all-around basketball players in the game, and undoubtedly he was the best backcourt player."

Put a ball in Cousy's hand and one could not anticipate the next move. It might go behind his back, between his legs, nobody knew. And frequently this led to a basket for Cousy or the Celtics. Of course, a lot of people thought Cousy was showboating, but they were wrong. "Actually," he said, "I don't use the behind-the-back pass as often as people think I do. When I use it, I have a good reason for it. When a situation develops where I can help the club with a certain maneuver, I go ahead with it."

Cousy came to the Celtics after a brilliant college career at Holy Cross. The year was 1950. Thirteen seasons later, he retired and when he did, he left behind a set of statistics which serves as a standard for a backcourtman. For example, he once held the all-time league record for most minutes played (30,230) and he held the NBA record for most assists (6,949). When he retired, he was the fourth leading scorer in

Boston's masterful Bob Cousy made All-NBA 10 consecutive years.

NBA history (16,955 points) and was second in total games played (917). He also was named to the all-league team for 10 successive seasons. And he was the only player to participate in 13 All-Star games. In 1962, a poll of sports editors of 100 major daily papers named Cousy the NBA's all-time number one player.

Cousy was hired to coach the Cincinnati Royals before the 1969–70 season. In an attempt to bolster sagging attendance in Cincinnati and also to lend a steadying hand to the Royals' backcourt, he reactivated himself as a player. He appeared in seven games, scoring five points. But he did show some of his old playmaking skills by accumulating ten assists in just 34 minutes of playing time.

Cousy also demonstrated decisiveness as a coach by trading longtime Cincinnati stars Jerry Lucas and Oscar Robertson for lesser-known, younger players.

It is hard to pick Cousy's greatest feat. He once scored 50 points in a game, but some of his other contributions were even greater, though the amount of points was not as high. There was a game in Madison Square Garden in 1954 when the New York Knickerbockers were leading 93-89 with 30 seconds remaining. Cousy stole the ball twice within the 30 seconds and the Celtics forced an overtime. Then another. Finally they won, Cousy having scored 12 of the 20 points in overtime.

Or there was another time in New York — when he dribbled the ball so cunningly and killed the clock for the last 23 seconds of the game. Nobody could stop him. The next day, Jimmy Cannon of the New York *Journal-American* wrote, "If Cousy never put the ball in the basket, he'd still be the most respected man in the league. At the finish, Boston had a one-point lead with 23 seconds to play. It was then that Bob proved his greatness. He held onto the ball . . . dribbling it among the Knicks, scampering among them in a wild solo. He ran in a lunging crouch, his body bent to protect the ball from their hands, a thrilling dwarf among the frustrated giants."

COUSY, BOB

b. Aug. 9, 1928   Ht. 6-1   Wt. 175

College — Holy Cross

YR.	TEAM	G	FG	FT	TP	AVG.
1950–51	Boston	69	401	276	1078	15.6
1951–52	Boston	66	512	409	1433	21.7
1952–53	Boston	71	464	479	1407	19.8
1953–54	Boston	72	486	411	1383	19.2
1954–55	Boston	71	522	460	1504	21.2
1955–56	Boston	72	440	476	1356	18.8
1956–57	Boston	64	478	363	1319	20.6
1957–58	Boston	65	445	277	1167	18.0
1958–59	Boston	65	484	329	1297	20.0
1959–60	Boston	75	568	319	1455	19.4
1960–61	Boston	76	513	352	1378	18.1
1961–62	Boston	75	462	251	1175	15.7
1962–63	Boston	76	392	219	1003	13.2
1969–70	Cincinnati	7	1	3	5	0.7
	Totals	924	6168	4624	16960	18.4

8. JOE FULKS: Link to the Moderns

UPI

Joe Fulks was the man who focused the attention of the world on professional basketball. For when he was at his best, the game was still developing and basketball was not considered a high-scoring game. But Joe Fulks changed that and he changed many other things, too. He was the link between the prewar days and the modern era of professional basketball.

When Eddie Gottlieb, the coach and owner of the Philadelphia Warriors, signed him to a contract in 1946, he told the press: "We have a fellow by the name of Joe Fulks. You've probably never heard of him but I believe he has the potentialities of a great scorer."

Even Gottlieb did not realize how deep that potential was. In his first year, Fulks led the league in scoring with what then was considered an astounding average of 23.2 points per game (1,389 points in 60 contests). The Warriors won the World's Championship that season and the name Joe Fulks became synonymous with professional basketball.

Fulks was 24 when he started playing with the pros after serving with the Marines during World War II. He played only through the 1953–54 season, finishing his career with 8,003 points.

A graduate of Murray State College in Kentucky, Fulks was a slim 6-5, 190 pounds. His twisting pivot shots were the forerunner of the jump shot. His greatest feat came against the Indianapolis Jets at the Philadelphia Arena, February 10, 1949, when he electrified the sports world by scoring a record 63 points in one game. At that time, many teams did not score 63 points in a whole game.

That night, he shot spinning one-handers, running shots with either hand and his soft, looping set shots. They all worked. Only four players in the history of the game have scored 63 points or higher in a professional basketball game: Fulks, Wilt Chamberlain, Elgin Baylor, and Jerry West.

Joe Fulks was the first of the great scorers.

Despite his great scoring ability — when he retired, only George Mikan had scored more points — Fulks was often criticized. But even the critics had to admit his value to the Warriors. John (Honey) Russell, then coach of the Boston Celtics, once said: "Fulks is slow and he's not a great defensive player. And how can he be a great team player when he takes so many shots? But I wish I had him. I'd sure build my team around him."

Fulks viewed all the publicity and acclaim quite realistically. "They give me the ball and I shoot. That's all there is to it." That's an oversimplification, of course. Joe Fulks was a great basketball player and the game owes much of its early success to him.

FULKS, JOSEPH (Jumpin' Joe)
Ht. 6-5   Wt. 190
College — Murray State

YR.	TEAM	G	FG	FT	TP	AVG.
1946–47	Philadelphia	60	475	439	1389	23.2
1947–48	Philadelphia	43	326	297	949	22.1
1948–49	Philadelphia	60	529	502	1560	26.0
1949–50	Philadelphia	68	336	293	965	14.2
1950–51	Philadelphia	66	429	378	1236	18.7
1951–52	Philadelphia	61	336	250	922	15.1
1952–53	Philadelphia	70	332	168	832	11.9
1953–54	Philadelphia	61	61	28	150	2.5
Totals		489	2824	2355	8003	16.4

Neil Johnston: Man with a hook.

UPI

Neil Johnston was another victim of the George Mikan era. And though he was a three-time scoring champion, he could never break through and win the national acceptance that Mikan had. Eddie Gottlieb, who coached Johnston in Philadelphia, said, "I doubt if Johnston will ever receive the recognition that Mikan got because Neil didn't come into the league with the fanfare and blowing of trumpets that accompanied Mikan."

Johnston was an Ohio State graduate and a 6-8 center whose hook shot was a work of art. He also was accurate with a one-hander from the outside. In eight seasons, from 1952 through 1959, he scored 10,023 points and had an average of 19.4 points per game. He won the scoring title in successive seasons. In 1951–52 he scored 1,564 points for a 22.3 average; in 1953–54 he scored 1,759 for a 24.4 average; and in 1954–55 he had 1,631 points for 22.7.

He was just as adept at shooting and rebounding, winning the shooting percentage title three times (.452, .457 and .447). He won the rebounding title in 1954–55 with 1,085. For two seasons — 1952–53, 1953–54 — he led the league in most minutes played.

He might have been even greater, but a knee injury cut his career short when he was only 30 years old and still had some good years left. Despite the knee trouble, he tried to play. "On one good leg," said Al Cervi, one of his coaches with the Warriors, "he's better than some of the other men in this league. When he's out of the lineup it just kills us."

Finally, the knee no longer could stand the pain and the rigors of the rugged NBA schedule. Johnston had to end his outstanding career in 1959. He had made the NBA All-Star first team four times. When he retired, he was named coach of the Warriors just when another pretty good center, Wilt Chamberlain, was breaking in. Johnston remained as Warrior coach for two years. He was a frustrated man who had to watch from the bench instead of being out on the court playing.

JOHNSTON, NEIL

b. Feb. 4, 1929   Ht. 6-8   Wt. 215
College — Ohio State

YR.	TEAM	G	FG	FT	TP	AVG.
1951–52	Philadelphia	64	141	100	382	6.0
1952–53	Philadelphia	70	504	556	1564	22.3
1953–54	Philadelphia	72	591	577	1759	24.4
1954–55	Philadelphia	72	521	589	1631	22.7
1955–56	Philadelphia	70	499	549	1547	22.1
1956–57	Philadelphia	69	520	535	1575	22.8
1957–58	Philadelphia	71	473	442	1388	19.5
1958–59	Philadelphia	28	54	69	177	6.3
	Totals	516	3303	3417	10023	19.4

UPI

Some called him Easy Ed because of his modest, easygoing temperament. But he really earned the nickname on the basketball court, where he made his driving layups and virtually unstoppable hook shots look as easy as pushing a button.

Actually Ed Macauley had to develop his graceful smoothness almost out of necessity. At 6-8 and only 190 pounds, he just wasn't strong enough to battle some of the beefier NBA players. So Macauley concentrated on playmaking and shooting and it paid off. In nine and a fraction seasons in the league, Macauley made the All-NBA first team three times and the second team once and established himself as one of the all-time great NBA centers.

He graduated from St. Louis University in 1949 as a two-time All-American and signed a two-year contract for a reported $30,000 with the hometown St. Louis Bombers, who were struggling to stay in business. Macauley had a good rookie year, averaging 16.1 points a game, fifth best in the league, but the Bombers folded after the season ended.

The New York Knicks thought so much of Easy Ed that they offered to buy the entire St. Louis franchise just to obtain Macauley. But the NBA vetoed the transaction and the next season Macauley wound up with the Boston Celtics. Along with Bob Cousy and Bill Sharman, Macauley helped make the pro game a success in Boston.

Macauley played in the All-Star Game seven times and always did well. He was, in fact, the outstanding player in the very first All-Star Game in 1951. Three years later, in 1954, he was the only unanimous selection for the All-Star Game.

Macauley played six seasons for the Celtics and always finished among the league leaders in scoring. Over that span, he never averaged less than 17.5 points a game. More than merely a gunner, he usually finished among the leaders in field-goal accuracy, too.

On March 6, 1953, he had the greatest scoring night

Easy Ed Macauley (22) made it look easy.

of his career, riddling the Minneapolis Lakers with their great center, George Mikan, for 46 points.

For the 1956–57 season, Easy Ed moved back to St. Louis, his hometown. Ben Kerner, the owner of the St. Louis Hawks, had the draft rights to Bill Russell. But he felt that Russell, who had been a great college star at San Francisco, would probably sign with the Harlem Globetrotters after returning from the Olympic Games. So Kerner traded the rights to Russell to the Celtics in return for Macauley and Cliff Hagan.

Macauley, Bob Pettit, and Hagan led the Hawks to two consecutive Western Division titles and in 1957–58 the Hawks beat Boston for the NBA championship. Early in the next season Easy Ed retired as a player and took over as coach and general manager of the Hawks. In the two seasons he coached the Hawks, they won two Western titles. But he resigned in 1962 in order to devote more time to outside business interests.

In his years in the NBA, Macauley proved that a player didn't have to be a brute to be a good NBA center. He showed that agility and coordination were at least as important as sheer strength. Macauley made the game look easy — for himself and the fans who watched him, but never for the opponents who had to stop him.

MACAULEY, EDWARD (Easy Ed)						
b. Mar. 22, 1928 Ht. 6-8 Wt. 190						
College — St. Louis						
YR.	TEAM	G	FG	FT	TP	AVG.
1949–50	St. Louis	67	351	379	1081	16.1
1950–51	Boston	68	459	466	1384	20.4
1951–52	Boston	66	384	496	1264	19.2
1952–53	Boston	69	451	500	1402	20.3
1953–54	Boston	71	462	420	1344	18.9
1954–55	Boston	71	403	442	1248	17.6
1955–56	Boston	71	420	400	1240	17.5
1956–57	St. Louis	72	414	359	1187	16.5
1957–58	St. Louis	72	376	267	1019	14.2
1958–59	St. Louis	14	22	21	65	4.6
	Totals	641	3742	3750	11234	17.5

George Mikan vs. the All-Stars.

UPI

When analyzing George Mikan's position in the history of basketball, you must consider only the era he played: the late 1940s and early 1950s. This was before Wilt Chamberlain and Bill Russell.

Until the emergence of Chamberlain and Russell, Mikan had been considered the greatest big man in the game's history. But it is unfair to compare him with Chamberlain and Russell because they were different types completely.

George Mikan did much to revolutionize the game. And he did a lot to make the NBA a major league attraction because he was the main reason the Minneapolis Lakers won five World Championships. Mikan was so good during his time that when every other possible defense against him, fair or foul, had been tried and found wanting, the NBA was forced to widen the lanes under the basket from six to 12 feet.

During Mikan's heyday — and that of the Lakers — he dominated the record book. The 6-10 center from DePaul University scored 44 points or more in nine different games. His best effort was 61 points against the Rochester Royals in 1952. At one point, he held the all-time seasonal scoring average of 28.4 points per game. In his six big seasons with the Lakers — from 1948 to 1954 — he led the league in scoring three times, was second twice, and fourth in his last and worst year. He made the league All-Star first team each of the six years.

Mikan's size (245 pounds) also made him a target for the opposition. Each of his legs was broken once. His right foot, the arch of his left foot, his right wrist, his nose, and one thumb also were broken at one time or another. Three of his fingers were broken, too. His nose was ripped open by swinging elbows. He received a total of 166 stitches.

When Mikan first announced his retirement after the 1954 season, the basketball community was stunned and saddened. Of course, they realized he could not go on forever. Johnny Kundla, the Lakers' coach, was glum when he heard Mikan's plans. But later Kundla confessed to the press: "This should even up our league."

He was right. Mikan had dominated the game. Nobody was able to handle Number 99 during those years. Mikan stuck to his retirement for a year, but in the middle of the 1955–56 season he decided to try a comeback. It was not a success. He scored only 390 points in 37 games and when he retired for good at the end of the year, he left the NBA with 11,764 points and a 22.6 average.

Perhaps the greatest tribute paid Mikan was in New York at Madison Square Garden. It was not the size of the crowd nor was it a special night where he received a number of gifts. It was just a simple message on the marquee outside the Garden. All it said was:

Tonite
George Mikan
vs.
Knicks

MIKAN, GEORGE
b. June 18, 1924   Ht. 6-10   Wt. 245
College — DePaul

YR.	TEAM	G	FG	FT	TP	AVG.
1946–47	Chicago NL	25	147	119	413	16.5
1947–48	Minneapolis NL	56	406	383	1195	21.3
1948–49	Minneapolis	60	583	532	1698	28.3
1949–50	Minneapolis	68	649	567	1865	27.4
1950–51	Minneapolis	68	678	576	1932	28.4
1951–52	Minneapolis	64	545	433	1523	23.8
1952–53	Minneapolis	70	500	442	1442	20.6
1953–54	Minneapolis	72	441	424	1306	18.1
1955–56	Minneapolis	37	148	94	390	10.5
Totals		520	4097	3570	11764	22.6

UPI

The Minneapolis Lakers were the first team to dominate professional basketball. There were three big reasons: George Mikan, Jim Pollard, and a rugged 6-7, 230-pound forward named Vern Mikkelsen.

Over the years, Mikkelsen was one of the NBA's most consistent players. His teammates thought so highly of him that he served consecutive terms as captain for six seasons. Mikkelsen joined the Lakers in 1950 after playing collegiate ball at little-known Hamline College where he excelled off the court as much as on it. At Hamline, he earned a master of arts degree. He played 10 years for the Lakers including the glory years when they won three championships in his first four years. Mikkelsen was never a sensational scorer like teammate George Mikan. Consistency was his forte. When he completed his career, he was one of the game's leading scorers with 10,063 points in 700 games, an average of 14.4 points per game.

The balding Dane was a center in college but made the transition to forward when he joined the Lakers, who had a pretty fair center in Mikan. Teaming with Mikan and Pollard in the early days at Minneapolis, Mikkelsen helped initiate a new concept of play: three big men with two little ones.

He was extremely strong under the boards and on the court his rugged features and appearance belied the placid nature underneath. Mikkelsen, extremely erudite, had been a school teacher and had been selected to make a State Department expedition to Scandinavia.

On the court, however, he often wore his opponents down. He seldom missed a game and during one six-year stretch he missed only one game. Four times he was selected to the NBA's All-Star team. He was rough on the court and has the dubious distinction of fouling out of the most NBA games (127).

But he will be remembered because he was such an integral part of one of the world's greatest teams.

Vern Mikkelsen: A steady 10,000-point man.

He never received the publicity Mikan did, or even as much as Pollard. But his contributions were just as important. He might have lasted longer as a professional, but inception of the 24-second rule hurt. It was not tailored to the bulkier, slower giants and the type of ball control the old Lakers favored.

After the Lakers won the NBA title for the fifth time in 1954, Maurice Podoloff, commissioner of the league, paid Mikkelsen and the Lakers the ultimate tribute. "I will say it was the greatest team in the history of basketball and deserves a place not earned by any team in any other type of athletics. The Lakers have been the greatest contributing factor to the success of the NBA."

MIKKELSON, VERN
b. Oct. 21, 1928   Ht. 6-7   Wt. 230
College — Hamline

YR.	TEAM	G	FG	FT	TP	AVG.
1949–50	Minneapolis	68	288	215	791	11.6
1950–51	Minneapolis	64	359	186	904	14.1
1951–52	Minneapolis	66	363	283	1009	15.3
1952–53	Minneapolis	70	378	291	1047	15.0
1953–54	Minneapolis	72	288	221	797	11.1
1954–55	Minneapolis	71	440	447	1327	18.7
1955–56	Minneapolis	72	317	328	962	13.4
1956–57	Minneapolis	72	322	342	986	13.7
1957–58	Minneapolis	72	439	370	1248	17.3
1958–59	Minneapolis	72	353	286	992	13.8
	Totals	699	3547	2969	10063	14.4

Bob Pettit: 20,880 points.

13. BOB PETTIT: Head of the Class

MALCOLM EMMONS

They said he was too skinny. Too light. He would not hold up as a corner man in the National Basketball Association. Bob Pettit listened politely to the evaluation. And he smiled. He had just been graduated from Louisiana State and had been drafted by the Milwaukee Hawks.

The 6-9, 215-pound Pettit reported to the Hawks in 1954 and that first year scored 1,466 points for a 20.4 average. That ended the doubt and the speculation. The following year, Bob Pettit was even more sensational. The Hawks had moved to St. Louis and Pettit made the game a success there by winning the scoring title (1,849 points) and rebounding title (1,164). He also won the Most Valuable Player Award and was selected as the MVP in the All-Star Game. You can go on and on listing Bob Pettit's records and achievements.

It would not be an overstatement to say he may have been the best frontcourtman ever to play professional basketball. He won the MVP award twice, the scoring title twice and the rebounding title once. Four times he was selected as the outstanding performer in the All-Star Game, and he was named to the All-NBA team 10 years in a row. He was a pleasure to watch: a smooth shooter with an exceedingly accurate jump shot, a deceptive rebounder who used finesse to outwit and out-rebound stronger men.

Pettit ranks as the fourth leading scorer in the history of the NBA. He played 11 years, scoring 20,880 points in 792 games for a lifetime average of 26.4. That scoring average was the fifth best in the league's history. He also ranked second in minutes played until Chamberlain overtook him. And he was the league's third leading rebounder (12,851). He had six games in which he scored more than 50 points including a career high of 57 in 1961. Until Elgin Baylor broke the record, Pettit also was the leading scorer in playoff history.

Off the court, Pettit was all class. The same as he was in uniform. He had an inordinate amount of pride. "What it is with me, I guess," he said, "is that as you go along in life and work hard, you reach new plateaus of accomplishment. With each plateau you reach, the demands upon you become greater. And your pride increases to meet the demands. You drive yourself harder than before. You can't afford negative thinking, so you always believe you'll win. You build an image of yourself that has nothing to do with ego — but it has to be satisfied. When I fall below what I know I can do, my belly growls and growls. Anytime I'm not playing up to my very best I can count on a jolt of indigestion."

Bob Pettit had a unique barometer. But judging from the record, he could not have suffered too badly.

PETTIT, BOB

b. Dec. 12, 1932   Ht. 6-9   Wt. 215

College — Louisiana State

YR.	TEAM	G	FG	FT	TP	AVG.
1954–55	Milwaukee	72	520	426	1466	20.4
1955–56	St. Louis	72	646	557	1849	25.7
1956–57	St. Louis	71	613	529	1755	24.7
1957–58	St. Louis	70	581	557	1719	24.6
1958–59	St. Louis	72	719	667	2105	29.2
1959–60	St. Louis	72	669	544	1882	26.1
1960–61	St. Louis	76	769	582	2120	27.9
1961–62	St. Louis	78	867	695	2429	31.1
1962–63	St. Louis	79	778	685	2241	28.4
1963–64	St. Louis	80	791	608	2190	27.4
1964–65	St. Louis	50	396	332	1124	22.5
	Totals	792	7349	6182	20880	26.4

14. JIM POLLARD: Corner Man

UPI

In 1952, the players who had been in the National Basketball Association since its inception as the BAA voted in a poll to determine who was the best player of the period. The winner was Jim Pollard, the front-courtman for the Minneapolis Lakers. To win the poll, Pollard finished ahead of such greats as teammate George Mikan and Joe Fulks.

It was a wonderful tribute to a player who contributed as much to the success of the Lakers as the high-scoring Mikan. Of course, Pollard never received the publicity Mikan did. Pollard was not a high scorer like Mikan. He averaged 13.1 points per game during his eight-year career and scored 6,522 points. But he was the classic team player. "You can get a lot of points in a game," he once said, "and still be dissatisfied with yourself. After all, it isn't an individual record you're after, but a victory."

Pollard's best weapon was his jump shot. Together with Vern Mikkelsen and Mikan he helped the Lakers dominate the game in those early years. Mikkelsen, Mikan, and Pollard were the best one-two-three punch the game had seen.

You can get a better picture of Pollard when you listen to the comments some of his fellow pros made when the poll was taken. Said Fred Scolari of the Fort Wayne Pistons: "Pollard can do more things than anyone. He is better than most big men and decidedly better than the little men. He's been in the shade of Mikan. He is a basketball players' player all the way."

Bones McKinney, another Pollard opponent, had tremendous respect for him, too. "Pollard," McKinney said, "was the greatest corner man ever. On another club no one would touch him. He can do everything on a basketball floor and do it with finesse."

Finesse is important when you speak of Jim Pollard. He seldom made the wrong move. And he was consistent. His playoff scoring average was 13.4, three tenths of a point above his career average.

Jim Pollard: Mr. Clean.

Another interesting statistic: Pollard was considered one of the cleanest players in basketball and in one three-year stretch committed only 194 personal fouls. He was a graduate of Stanford University. Later he coached the Lakers for a brief period before becoming a college coach.

POLLARD, JIM
Ht. 6-3   Wt. 190
College — Stanford

YR.	TEAM	G	FG	FT	TP	AVG.
1947–48	·Minneapolis NL	59	310	140	760	12.9
1948–49	Minneapolis	53	314	156	784	14.8
1949–50	Minneapolis	66	394	185	973	14.7
1950–51	Minneapolis	54	256	117	629	11.6
1951–52	Minneapolis	65	411	183	1005	15.5
1952–53	Minneapolis	66	333	193	859	13.0
1953–54	Minneapolis	71	326	179	831	11.7
1954–55	Minneapolis	63	265	151	681	10.8
	Totals	497	2609	1304	6522	13.1

Frank Ramsey (23) was pioneer supersub.

15. FRANK RAMSEY: Supersub

Frank Ramsey started the trend. Nowadays most successful professional teams rely on the valuable "sixth starter" who can come into a game and break it open in a matter of minutes.

Ramsey was the first one. He played for the Boston Celtics in the mid-1950's and early 1960's. "He is the most versatile player in the league," his coach, Red Auerbach, said. "He can come off the bench and do the job of either a big man or little man for me and grows cooler as the game grows more tense."

In nine seasons, Ramsey scored 8,378 points for a 13.4 average. Those figures may not seem impressive but Ramsey was a substitute most of that time. "I'd rather be a sub on a great team than a regular on a losing one," he said. "Even a spare part feels sort of special when a fine mechanism like the Celtics is involved."

The Celtics would go to Ramsey when they needed a quick spark. He could, as Auerbach said, play anywhere and do the job needed. "He's the one," said teammate Bob Cousy, "who has kept us up in the standings because he's versatile and steady, a real producer."

Ramsey was a product of Adolph Rupp and the University of Kentucky. And he became as integral a part of the Celtic dynasty as any of the starters. His best season was 1957–58 when he averaged 16.5 points per game. The next four seasons he was extremely consistent, averaging 15 points per game each season. He was at his best in the playoffs and in four straight seasons (1958 through 1961) averaged the following: 18.4, 23.2, 18.1, and 17.1.

Soon other teams around the league began to learn the value of the "sixth starter." When Ramsey retired, John Havlicek assumed that role for the Celtics. Billy Cunningham was the same type of player for the Philadelphia 76ers.

Havlicek and Cunningham scored more than Ramsey, but Frank was the pathfinder. Today a specialist like Ramsey is all important. As Ramsey's teammate,

Bill Russell, said, "He does the thing that has to be done to win a game." Ramsey won quite a few for the Celtics during his nine seasons in the league.

RAMSEY, FRANK
b. July 13, 1931   Ht. 6-3   Wt. 190
College — Kentucky

YR.	TEAM	G	FG	FT	TP	AVG.
1954–55	Boston	64	236	243	715	11.2
1956–57	Boston	35	137	144	418	11.9
1957–58	Boston	69	377	383	1137	16.5
1958–59	Boston	72	383	341	1107	15.4
1959–60	Boston	73	422	273	1117	15.3
1960–61	Boston	79	448	295	1191	15.1
1961–62	Boston	79	436	334	1206	15.3
1962–63	Boston	77	284	271	839	10.9
1963–64	Boston	75	226	196	648	8.6
Totals		623	2949	2480	8378	13.4

16. OSCAR ROBERTSON: Big O

There is a story Tom Meschery, the veteran NBA forward, enjoyed telling when asked about Oscar Robertson's myriad talents. "We were playing Cincinnati and Earl Strom was one of the officials. Somehow I wound up guarding Oscar after a switch. Well, Oscar throws that ball behind his back, heads for the basket, and leaves me behind. It was a fantastic move, split-second like always with him. Just as the ball goes in, Strom calls walking. Oscar gets real excited and starts screaming at him, 'How can you call that walking, you never saw that move before.'"

Oscar probably was right, but the official prevailed. Some of the moves he has made throughout his career have been unbelievable. As they say in the NBA: "Never turn your head on Oscar, there is no telling what he might show you next. His body control is even more amazing than his shooting touch."

Red Auerbach, the former Boston coach, is one of Robertson's greatest admirers. "There is nothing he can't do," Auerbach said. "No one comes close to him or has the ability to break open a game as Oscar. He's so great he scares me. He can beat you all by himself and usually does."

Robertson, 6-5 and weighing 220 pounds, was an All-American at the University of Cincinnati before joining the Cincinnati Royals in 1960–61 when he promptly showed his greatness with a 30.5 scoring average. The third leading scorer in NBA history, Robertson's career mark is more than 29 points per game.

He also is considered one of the greatest playmakers in history and holds the league record for highest assist average in a season (11.5 in 1964–65). Robertson won the assist title seven times in his first ten seasons. He was the league's leading foul shooter twice — in 1963–64 (.853) and 1967–68 (.873).

Oscar, of course, holds virtually every Cincinnati Royals record. He was the team's leading scorer for ten consecutive seasons (1961–70), its best playmaker

The Big O.

(1961–70). He also led in minutes played for six seasons and twice pulled the incredible feat of also leading the Royals in rebounds.

Following the 1969–70 season, Robertson was traded to the Milwaukee Bucks for Flynn Robinson and Charlie Paulk. Bob Cousy, the Cincinnati coach, earlier in the season had attempted to trade Oscar to the Baltimore Bullets. But Robertson vetoed that trade, pointing to a special clause in his contract that gave him the right of approval over all trades involving him. He seemed happier, however, about joining the Bucks and teaming with Lew Alcindor, their great young center.

He will be remembered best for his versatility. There was nothing beyond his talent — or imagination — on the basketball floor. Three times (1961, 1964, 1969) he was named the Most Valuable Player at the NBA All-Star Game, and he played in the game each year he was in the league.

In a poll of sports editors of the nation's 100 largest newspapers, the Academy of Sports selected Robertson on the all-time NBA team. He received 51 percent of the voting points, only two points behind Wilt Chamberlain.

ROBERTSON, OSCAR (The Big O)						
b. Nov. 24, 1938 Ht. 6-5 Wt. 205						
College — Cincinnati						
YR.	TEAM	G	FG	FT	TP	AVG.
1960–61	Cincinnati	71	756	653	2165	30.5
1961–62	Cincinnati	79	866	700	2432	30.8
1962–63	Cincinnati	80	825	614	2264	28.3
1963–64	Cincinnati	79	840	800	2480	31.4
1964–65	Cincinnati	75	807	665	2279	30.4
1965–66	Cincinnati	76	818	742	2378	31.3
1966–67	Cincinnati	79	838	736	2412	30.5
1967–68	Cincinnati	65	660	576	1896	29.2
1968–69	Cincinnati	79	656	643	1955	24.7
1969–70	Cincinnati	69	647	454	1748	25.3
	Totals	752	7713	6583	22009	29.3

Bill Russell set the standards for defense.

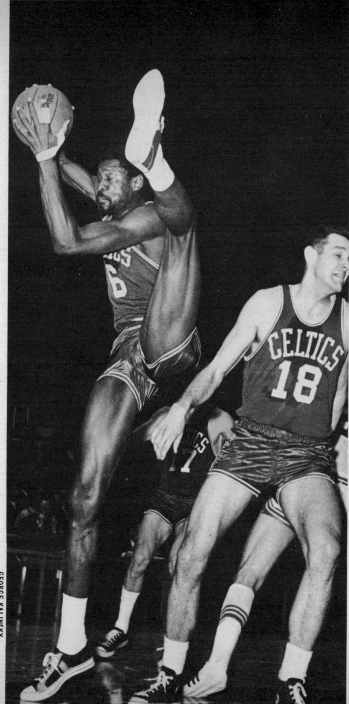

GEORGE KALINSKY

If a player's value is measured by the number of championships he helps his team win, then Bill Russell must be considered the greatest player in the history of basketball.

Certainly no one will quarrel with the statement that he was the best defensive player in the game's history. In fact, he completely revolutionized professional basketball and brought back the emphasis on defense. And in doing so, he led the Boston Celtics to 11 World Championships in 13 years.

Standing 6-10 and weighing 220 pounds, Russell entered the NBA during the 1956–57 season following a sensational college career at the University of San Francisco where he led his team to a pair of national championships.

He didn't change his winning habits when he turned professional. His forte was rebounding. Until Wilt Chamberlain broke it, Russell held the individual game rebounding record with 51. On two other occasions Russell gathered in 49 rebounds in a game. He led the league in rebounding four different times, and was named Most Valuable Player five times.

Russell never was a great scorer — his lifetime average being 15.1 points per game. Nor was he an outstanding shooter from the field or foul line. It was on defense where he caused the opposition so much trouble. And he was well-paid for it, reaching the $100,000 class and approaching the $200,000 class.

Too bad the NBA did not keep statistics for shots blocked or broken plays. Russell would have led in both departments. Opposing centers often could not sleep the night before they had to face Russell in the pivot. Some of Russell's greatest duels were against Chamberlain, and Chamberlain provides the final commentary on that rivalry with the statement: "I've been in eight playoffs with Boston where it came down to the final game and Boston won seven."

It is also interesting to note that Russell scored at a somewhat accelerated pace (16.2) throughout his playoff career and his rebounding also was better during this period. He will be remembered as one of the game's greatest "money" players. During the 1965–66 playoffs, for example, he grabbed 428 rebounds in 17 games for an average of 25.1 rebounds per game.

The only years during his career when the Celtics did not win the World Championship were 1957–58 and 1966–67. His finest year, however, may have been 1967–68. The Celtics finished second that year in the season's standings behind Philadelphia. In the opening round of the playoffs, they had a tough time against the Detroit Pistons. Their age, the experts claimed, was beginning to show. They were heavy underdogs when they met the 76ers for the Eastern Division championship.

Down three games to one in the best-of-seven series, Russell took command and led the Celtics to a stunning comeback. He mastered Chamberlain completely in the seventh game, holding him to a mere two shots in the second half.

In 1966, Russell took over as player-coach of the Celtics following Red Auerbach's retirement. When the Celtics failed to win the title that first year, Russell's job was considered in jeopardy. But Boston came back to win championships the next two seasons before Russell retired as both player and coach in 1969.

The final word on Russell's value to the Celtics can be found in the team's performance the year after his retirement. World Champions in Russell's final season, Boston dropped all the way to sixth place without him.

RUSSELL, BILL
b. Feb. 12, 1934   Ht. 6-10   Wt. 220
College — San Francisco

YR.	TEAM	G	FG	FT	TP	AVG.
1956–57	Boston	48	277	152	706	14.7
1957–58	Boston	69	456	230	1142	16.6
1958–59	Boston	70	456	256	1168	16.7
1959–60	Boston	74	555	240	1350	18.2
1960–61	Boston	78	532	258	1322	16.9
1961–62	Boston	76	575	286	1436	18.9
1962–63	Boston	78	511	287	1309	16.8
1963–64	Boston	78	466	236	1168	15.0
1964–65	Boston	78	429	244	1102	14.1
1965–66	Boston	78	391	223	1005	12.9
1966–67	Boston	81	395	285	1075	13.4
1967–68	Boston	78	365	247	977	12.5
1968–69	Boston	77	279	204	762	9.9
Totals		963	5687	3148	14522	15.1

Dolph Schayes: Wherever the action was.

18. DOLPH SCHAYES: Iron Man

UPI

There once was a team, a wonderful team, that night after night gave the simplest, most exciting display of pure basketball ever seen in the National Basketball Association. It wasn't a big team and it did not have a roster full of All-Americans or towering frontcourtmen. What the Syracuse Nationals did have was a distinct spirit and a forward named Dolph Schayes.

Schayes personified the spirit of the Nats. Each time he scored a goal, he would run to the opposite end of the court, fist clenched triumphantly above his head. From the start, when he made Rookie of the Year in 1949, Schayes was one of the league's class players. When he retired at the end of the 1964 season, he was the all-time leading scorer with 19,249 points (18.2). His place in NBA history is secure. Schayes was 6-8 and a forward, but he was such a versatile performer that he was one of the last of the deadly two-hand set shooters. This helped make him great. He could score from the outside as easily as he could drive underneath for a layup.

One got a complete picture of Dolph Schayes the competitor when listening to him speak following his 29th birthday: "I feel I can still improve. Where? Defensively for one thing. And you can always become a better shot, can't you?"

Schayes was a rugged rebounder, winning the individual title in 1951 and finishing his career in fourth place on the all-time list. He was not afraid to become involved in the rough play under the boards and still holds the record for most personal fouls committed in league history (3,667). He also holds the record, however, for most foul shots made (6,979) which tells you even more about his competitive nature. He was a tireless performer, too, again ranking among the top ten in league history in minutes played (29,800).

It was hard to move Schayes out of the lineup. In 1952, he broke his right wrist. A cast was applied and Schayes continued to play. "The cast," he said in a typical Schayes statement, "made me work on my lefthanded shots, which soon improved. Later, when the left wrist was cracked, my righthanded shots improved."

Through the Nats won only one World Championship during Schayes' career, they never missed the playoffs and Schayes holds the league record for most playoff series (15). During that time he played in 103 playoff games.

Schayes' hustle has become legendary when people speak of and write about NBA history. He played with broken wrists, he played with other injuries, and he played when he was sick because he had to — for all those years — carry the burden of the Syracuse offense. Watching the Nationals play was a treat. They believed in the team game and patterned, but exciting, offense. And the most exciting, most dramatic individual on that team was Dolph Schayes.

SCHAYES, DOLPH
b. May 19, 1928   Ht. 6-8   Wt. 220
College — New York University

YR.	TEAM	G	FG	FT	TP	AVG.
1948–49	Syracuse NL	63	272	267	811	12.8
1949–50	Syracuse	64	348	376	1072	16.8
1950–51	Syracuse	66	332	457	1121	17.0
1951–52	Syracuse	63	263	342	868	13.8
1952–53	Syracuse	71	375	512	1262	17.8
1953–54	Syracuse	72	370	488	1228	17.1
1954–55	Syracuse	72	422	489	1333	18.5
1955–56	Syracuse	72	465	542	1472	20.4
1956–57	Syracuse	72	496	625	1617	22.5
1957–58	Syracuse	72	581	629	1791	24.9
1958–59	Syracuse	72	504	526	1534	21.3
1959–60	Syracuse	75	578	533	1689	22.5
1960–61	Syracuse	79	594	680	1868	23.6
1961–62	Syracuse	56	268	286	822	14.7
1962–63	Syracuse	66	223	181	627	9.5
1963–64	Philadelphia	24	44	46	134	5.6
	Totals	1059	6135	6979	19249	18.2

19. BILL SHARMAN: Robot Shooter

BOSTON CELTICS

When listing basketball's best shooters, Bill Sharman must be included. "Sharman," said Red Auerbach, his coach with the Celtics, "is the greatest shooter from the backcourt the game has ever seen." Eddie Gottlieb, the former owner and coach of the Philadelphia Warriors, watched Sharman destroy his team on many a cold winter night. "Sharman," he said, "must be listed with the all-time greats if only for his shooting ability."

Sharman and Bob Cousy formed the most potent backcourt in the history of basketball. If the defense let up on Sharman, Cousy would explode. If the defense was tough on Cousy, Bill Sharman — with his sure, deft touch — would start pumping those one-handers which made him famous. Sharman played 11 seasons for the Celtics, joining them for the 1950–51 season and retiring at the end of the 1961 season. He ranks among the top scorers in league history with 12,665 points in 710 games, a 17.8 average.

Oddly, Sharman never was considered an exceptional "long" shooter. His best scoring range was from 20 feet. Rarely did he attempt a shot from beyond that distance. Inside it, he was a sure bet. His career field goal percentage was .423, making him the best shooting guard of his time. Writer Dick Kaplan once said: "What made Sharman's shooting remarkable was its purity. He shot with almost robotlike precision, his style so polished and precise that it seemed like an illustration for a book on how to play basketball." Appropriately, Sharman did write a book on shooting, titled Sharman on Shooting.

Sharman and Cousy were with the Celtics when the Boston team was ripping off World Championship after World Championship. Though Cousy received most of the publicity, the NBA players recognized Sharman's abilities and voted him to the All-Star first team four different years. Sharman was recognized as the game's finest foul shooter and is the all-time

Bill Sharman was sharpest-shooting Celtic.

league leader in this department. During his career, he made 3,143 of 3,557 attempts for an .883 percentage. He won the foul shooting title seven different times.

A great natural athlete from the University of Southern California, Sharman almost had a major league baseball career. He was an outfielder in the Brooklyn Dodgers' system and was with the team at the end of the 1951 season when Bobby Thomson of the New York Giants hit the celebrated home run to give the Giants the pennant.

Luckily for Auerbach and the Celtics, Sharman chose basketball. There will be few to match him. He made shooting an art and can discuss it for hours. "I aim for the back rim," he said. "Why? I've found that most shots are missed 'short' because players get tired. Their shots start bouncing off that front rim. But if you shoot for the back rim, you get three factors working for you: First, most players shoot with backspin. If a backspinning ball hits the front rim, it skids away. But if it hits the back rim, the 'English' practically forces it into the basket. Second, if you overshoot and miss the back rim, you still have a chance for a cheap basket. The ball can bank in off the backboard. Third, the rim of the basket has an 18-inch diameter; the basketball about nine inches. So if you shoot for the rear rim, you have a nine-inch margin for error."

Sound like a science? It is. And Bill Sharman earned his doctorate.

SHARMAN, BILL
b. May 25, 1926   Ht. 6-1   Wt. 190
College — Southern California

YR.	TEAM	G	FG	FT	TP	AVG.
1950–51	Washington	31	141	96	378	12.2
1951–52	Boston	63	244	183	671	10.7
1952–53	Boston	71	403	341	1147	16.2
1953–54	Boston	72	412	331	1155	16.0
1954–55	Boston	68	453	347	1253	18.4
1955–56	Boston	72	538	358	1434	19.9
1956–57	Boston	67	516	381	1413	21.1
1957–58	Boston	63	550	302	1402	22.3
1958–59	Boston	72	562	342	1466	20.4
1959–60	Boston	71	599	252	1370	19.3
1960–61	Boston	60	383	210	976	16.3
	Totals	710	4761	3143	12665	17.8

20. JACK TWYMAN: More than a Player

MADISON SQUARE GARDEN

Red Auerbach, as Boston coach, had the best description of Jack Twyman. "Show him a little daylight," Auerbach said, "and it's up and in." Twyman was one of the great shooting forwards in the NBA and ranked eighth in the all-time scoring derby with a 19.2 average and 15,840 points during an 11-year career with the Rochester Royals and then the Cincinnati Royals.

From the very start, Twyman, an All-American at the University of Cincinnati, impressed people around the NBA. Bobby Wanzer, his coach at Rochester where he broke in, claimed that "Twyman has more determination than any player I've seen. He's the kind of guy who can key himself into things."

One can understand Twyman's dedication to shooting on hearing him explain his workout routine during the off-season. "I usually work out four days a week and during every session I shoot 100 fouls, 200 jump shots and between 100 and 150 set shots." He had some fantastic scoring years for the Royals but he never won a scoring championship. In 1958–59 he finished second to Bob Pettit in the scoring race and the following season, his best as a scorer, he averaged 31.2 points and finished second to Wilt Chamberlain.

For a corner man, Twyman had some outstanding shooting percentages. In 1960–61, he had a .488 average, in 1961–1962 it was .479 and the year after that .480. "You can feel it when you're hot," Twyman used to say. "You feel like everything you throw up there at the basket is going to drop through." In the case of Twyman, the shots fell through.

Twyman ranks in the all-time top twenty in a number of categories including most games played (823), most field goals scored (6,237), and most minutes played (26,055). He won the field goal percentage title in 1957–58 with a .452 average.

Jack Twyman (31) will be remembered for more than his playing.

But Twyman will be remembered for more than just his basketball talent. He was one of the great humanitarians — not just in sports, but in all walks of life. When his teammate Maurice Stokes was paralyzed with a brain ailment at the end of the 1958 season, Twyman became his legal guardian and raised funds for Maurice's treatment. Stokes' progress was slow but steady until he suffered a fatal heart attack in the spring of 1970. Each year while Stokes was hospitalized, NBA players had participated in a benefit game organized by Twyman for Stokes.

TWYMAN, JACK
b. May 11, 1934   Ht. 6-6   Wt. 210
College — Cincinnati

YR.	TEAM	G	FG	FT	TP	AVG.
1955–56	Rochester	72	417	204	1038	14.4
1956–57	Rochester	72	449	276	1174	16.3
1957–58	Cincinnati	72	465	307	1237	17.2
1958–59	Cincinnati	72	710	437	1857	25.8
1959–60	Cincinnati	75	870	598	2338	31.2
1960–61	Cincinnati	79	796	405	1997	25.3
1961–62	Cincinnati	80	739	353	1831	22.9
1962–63	Cincinnati	80	641	204	1586	19.8
1963–64	Cincinnati	68	447	189	1083	19.9
1964–65	Cincinnati	80	479	198	1156	14.5
1965–66	Cincinnati	73	224	95	543	7.4
Totals		823	6237	3366	15840	19.2

Jerry West: Greatest in the clutch.

LOS ANGELES LAKERS

Fred Schaus, who coached Jerry West at West Virginia University and later with the Los Angeles Lakers, has nothing but admiration for one of the finest guards ever to set foot on a basketball court.

Said Schaus: "If you sat down to build a 6-foot-3-inch basketball player you would come up with a Jerry West. He is the man that has everything — a fine shooting touch, speed, quickness, all the physical assets, including a tremendous dedication to the game." It was the perfect summation, and perhaps the last part of Schaus' statement was the most important. Jerry West's dedication made him great. Throughout his college career he had been compared with Oscar Robertson. Both broke into the NBA together. Oscar, however, got off to a sensational professional start, averaging 30.5 points per game as a rookie. West didn't do nearly as well, averaging 17.6. Immediately the doubters were saying "I told you so."

There was a lot of pressure, but the next season, Jerry West — through sheer determination — wound up with a 30.8 scoring average and from that point he was considered to be on the same level with Robertson. West is the sixth leading scorer in NBA history, a goal achieved despite the fact that he missed many games due to injuries.

"Jerry," said former Laker general manager Lou Mohs, "gets hurt a lot because he plays recklessly and doesn't spare himself." One of the oddities of sports is that West has suffered a broken nose eight times during his career, which says something for his gameness and willingness to mix it up under the boards despite his lack of size.

He has had some fine scoring seasons including a league-leading 31.2 in 1969–70 and a career high of 31.4 during the 1965–66 season. He has had some fantastic playoff series, including the 1964–65 season when he averaged 40.6 points for 11 games. The next season he averaged 34.2 in 14 games. Over his career, West has scored more points in playoffs than any other player in NBA history.

As coach of the Boston Celtics, Red Auerbach often became exasperated with West's performances against his teams. "You really can't stop West," Auerbach said. "You can try in a number of ways: play him loose, keep him away from the ball. Still he'll find a way to get his 25 to 30 points."

West's most effective weapon is a graceful jump shot from any spot on the floor. He is also an extremely good driver and an excellent playmaker. He is a perennial all-league selection and has been a yearly performer in the All-Star Game.

Despite all his records, one goal has always escaped West; he has never played on a championship team in his ten professional seasons. Seven times in that span the Lakers have made it into the playoff finals, only to fall short. Six times they lost to the Boston Celtics, and in 1969–70 it was the New York Knickerbockers who denied West and the Lakers the title.

WEST, JERRY

b. May 28, 1938   Ht. 6-3   Wt. 175

College — West Virginia

YR.	TEAM	G	FG	FT	TP	AVG.
1960–61	Los Angeles	79	529	331	1389	17.6
1961–62	Los Angeles	75	799	712	2310	30.8
1962–63	Los Angeles	56	559	371	1489	26.6
1963–64	Los Angeles	72	740	584	2064	28.7
1964–65	Los Angeles	74	822	648	2292	31.0
1965–66	Los Angeles	79	818	840	2476	31.4
1966–67	Los Angeles	66	645	602	1892	28.7
1967–68	Los Angeles	51	476	391	1343	26.3
1968–69	Los Angeles	61	545	490	1580	25.9
1969–70	Los Angeles	74	831	647	2309	31.2
Totals		687	6764	5116	19144	27.8

II
MODERN PRO HISTORY

22
NBA Yearly Roundups, Standings, Playoff Results, Individual Leaders

In the summer of 1946 owners of some of the nation's largest sports arenas became convinced that the time was right to bring major league professional basketball to the biggest cities. With the conclusion of World War II, many fine collegiate players were discharged from the Armed Forces and became available to the pro teams. In addition, the lifting of wartime restrictions on the economy left Americans with more money for entertainment.

The group of arena owners, led by Walter Brown, president of the Boston Garden, and Al Sutphin, owner of the Cleveland Arena, all had successfully promoted such events as ice hockey, ice shows, boxing, rodeos, and other sporting attractions. Encouraged by the drawing power of college basketball, they felt that a large potential audience for the professional game existed as well.

On June 6, 1946, these men met in New York City to organize a new major professional league, the Basketball Association of America. The owners chose Maurice Podoloff, a New Haven, Connecticut, lawyer, as president of the league. At the time Podoloff was president of the American Hockey League. Podoloff is given credit for holding the league together through its difficult early years. The BAA began play with teams in 11 cities: Boston, New York, Philadelphia, Providence, Toronto, Washington, Chicago, St. Louis, Cleveland, Detroit, and Pittsburgh.

To encourage an offense-minded game, the new league outlawed all varieties of zone defense. Only man-to-man defenses were permitted.

The National Basketball League, with most of its franchises in smaller Midwestern cities, had been in operation since the 1937–38 season, and the two leagues immediately embarked on a struggle for supremacy in professional basketball. The BAA and NBL competed for the services of the best graduating college players each season.

But before the 1948–49 season the BAA dealt the older league a crushing blow by picking up four of its best franchises, including Minneapolis with George Mikan. A year later the war was over. The two leagues merged to form a new 17-team circuit called the National Basketball Association. Podoloff was elected president of the NBA and Ike W. Duffey, who had headed the NBL, became chairman of the new league's Executive Board.

A detailed year-by-year history of the modern era in professional basketball, dating from the establishment of the Basketball Association of America in the 1946–47 season, follows:

UPI

Washington's Bones McKinney made the BAA's first All-Star team.

The established National Basketball League and the brand-new Basketball Association of America each unveiled a high-powered scorer this season. And each of these stars led his team to victory in the playoffs.

The Philadelphia Warriors, paced by Joe Fulks, won the first championship in the BAA, and the Chicago American Gears, with 6-10 George Mikan, won the NBL playoffs, although Rochester emerged as the NBL champion.

The BAA began play with 11 teams, divided into two divisions. In the East, the Washington Capitols, coached by Arnold "Red" Auerbach, finished the regular season 14 games ahead of Eddie Gottlieb's Philadelphia Warriors. The New York Knickerbockers, Providence Steamrollers, Toronto Huskies, and Boston Celtics followed.

The Western Division race was much closer, with the Chicago Stags finishing just one game ahead of the St. Louis Bombers. The Cleveland Rebels, Detroit Falcons and Pittsburgh Ironmen trailed. In the final series for the league championship, the Warriors crushed Chicago, four games to one. The crowd numbered 8,221 for the final playoff game in Philadelphia.

Fulks, a 6-6 exmarine, was the BAA's top individual performer. He earned the nickname "Jumpin' Joe" as he averaged 23.1 points a game and consistently outleaped taller opponents. Jumpin' Joe scored 41 points against Toronto, the highest individual total in the BAA's first season.

Fulks shot more times (1,557) — and scored more baskets (475) — than anyone else in the league. He finished with a lead of more than 400 points over his nearest rival, Bob Feerick of Washington.

Other top players included little 5-10 Ernie Calverley of Providence and Max Zaslofsky of Chicago. Calverley, who had played on the famous "point-a-minute" teams at Rhode Island State, led the league in assists and also finished sixth in scoring with a 14.3 average. Zaslofsky, who ignored the jump shot in favor of a two-hand set, was the fifth-leading scorer with a 14.4 average. Many of his points came on shots from beyond the 30-foot mark.

The first BAA All-Star team included Fulks, who was a unanimous selection, Feerick, Zaslofsky, Stan Miasek of Detroit, and Bones McKinney of Washington.

While Fulks was burning up the BAA, George Mikan, the giant from DePaul University, was making his pro debut with the NBL's Chicago Gears. The Gears, with player-coach Bobby McDermott and Mikan, who averaged 16.5 points, won the playoffs after finishing the regular season tied for third in the Western Division. A new league rule, however, gave the championship to the team with the best record for the entire season, and on this basis Rochester was declared the champion.

The NBL's All-Star team included Mikan, Mc-

Dermott, Fred Lewis of Sheboygan, and Al Cervi and Bob Davies of the Rochester Royals. Cervi, one of the few pros in the league who didn't go to college, was the NBL's leading scorer with a 14.4 average.

STANDINGS

EASTERN DIVISION

	W.	L.	Pct.
Washington	49	11	.817
Philadelphia	35	25	.583
New York	33	27	.550
Providence	28	32	.467
Toronto	22	38	.367
Boston	22	38	.367

WESTERN DIVISION

	W.	L.	Pct.
Chicago	39	22	.639
St. Louis	38	23	.623
Cleveland	30	30	.500
Detroit	20	40	.333
Pittsburgh	15	45	.250

PLAYOFFS

FIRST ROUND

Chicago defeated Washington 4 games to 2
Philadelphia defeated St. Louis 2 games to 1
New York defeated Cleveland 2 games to 1
Philadelphia defeated New York 2 games to 1

CHAMPIONSHIP

Philadelphia defeated Chicago 4 games to 1

TOP SCORERS

	Pts.	Ave.
Joe Fulks, Philadelphia	1389	23.2
Bob Feerick, Washington	926	16.8
Stan Miasek, Detroit	895	14.9
Ed Sadowski, Toronto-Cleveland	877	16.5
Max Zaslofsky, Chicago	877	14.4

LEADERS IN ASSISTS

	No.	Ave.
Ernie Calverley, Providence	202	3.4
Ken Sailors, Cleveland	134	2.3
Ossie Schectman, New York	109	2.0
Howie Dallmar, Philadelphia	104	1.7
Marv Rottner, Chicago	93	1.7

Philadelphia's Howie Dallmar drives on New York's Dick Holub.

1947-48

UPI

The Basketball Association of America lost four of its original franchises and added one new team for its second season. And it was the Baltimore Bullets, the new team, which provided the biggest surprise by winning the league championship.

The entire Western Division finished in almost a dead heat. St. Louis was first, with a 29-19 record, and the other three teams, Baltimore, Chicago, and Washington, finished in a three-way tie for second place, one game back. A special series of games had to be held to settle the final standings before the playoffs could get underway.

The Eastern Division race was close too, with the Philadelphia Warriors, the defending champions, finishing one game ahead of the New York Knicks. Toronto, Cleveland, Pittsburgh, and Detroit, all BAA members in the league's first season, had folded before the second campaign began, making it an eight-team circuit.

Baltimore came on in the playoffs and beat Philadelphia, four games to two, to win the league championship. Baltimore's player-coach, Buddy Jeanette, led the Bullets to the title with slick floor play and a 10.7 scoring average.

Philadelphia's Joe Fulks had the highest scoring average for the season, 22.1, but Chicago's Max Zaslofsky, with his long-range set shot, scored the most points, 1,009.

New York's Carl Braun, a 6-5 rookie from Colgate University, showed that he was a quick learner and one fine marksman when he shattered Fulks' single-game scoring mark of 41 points. Braun, a deadly outside shot, collected 47 points against Providence on December 6. Braun finished the season as the BAA's sixth-leading scorer with a 14.2 average.

Fulks, Max Zaslofsky of Chicago, and Bob Feerick of Washington all repeated as All-BAA selections. They were joined by Howie Dallmar of Philadelphia, the league leader in assists, and Ed Sadowski of Boston.

In the National Basketball League, Minneapolis, with George Mikan, won the playoff for the league title. The Lakers had taken over the franchise of Detroit, which had won only four games the previous season, but the addition of Mikan and Jim Pollard converted them into champions. Mikan, the NBL's Most Valuable Player, broke virtually all the league's scoring records as he averaged 21.3 points a game and reached a peak of 42 points against Syracuse. In the final playoff series, Minneapolis defeated Rochester, the defending champion, three games to one.

The All-NBL team included Mikan and Pollard of Minneapolis, Rookie of the Year Marko Todorovich of Sheboygan, and Al Cervi and Red Holzman of Rochester.

STANDINGS

EASTERN DIVISION

	W.	L.	Pct.
Philadelphia	27	21	.563
New York	26	22	.542
Boston	20	28	.417
Providence	6	42	.104

WESTERN DIVISION

	W.	L.	Pct.
St. Louis	29	19	.604
Baltimore	28	20	.583
Chicago	28	20	.583
Washington	28	20	.583

PLAYOFFS

FIRST ROUND

Philadelphia defeated St. Louis 4 games to 3
Baltimore defeated New York 2 games to 1
Chicago defeated Boston 2 games to 1
Baltimore defeated Chicago 2 games to 0

CHAMPIONSHIP

Baltimore defeated Philadelphia 4 games to 2

TOP SCORERS

	Pts.	Ave.
Max Zaslofsky, Chicago	1007	21.0
Joe Fulks, Philadelphia	949	22.1
Ed Sadowski, Boston	910	19.4
Bob Feerick, Washington	775	16.1
Stan Miasek, Chicago	716	14.9

LEADERS IN ASSISTS

	No.	Ave.
Howie Dallmar, Philadelphia	120	2.5
Ernie Calverley, Providence	119	2.5
Jim Seminoff, Chicago	89	1.8
Chuck Gilmur, Chicago	77	1.6
Ed Sadowski, Boston	74	1.6

Minneapolis, with George Mikan (99), won the title in its first year in the BAA.

UPI

1948-49

Disaster struck the old National Basketball League in midsummer as four of its best franchises switched to the Basketball Association of America. The NBL lost the Minneapolis Lakers and George Mikan, their great 6-10 center; Rochester; Fort Wayne and Indianapolis. These switches just about killed the NBL's chances for survival and left the pro basketball field virtually clear for the BAA.

Minneapolis and Mikan burst on the BAA scene with a vengeance. The Lakers won the league championship in their first season and Mikan used his tremendous strength and 240 pounds to great advantage. He dethroned Philadelphia's Joe Fulks, the BAA's resident scoring whiz, as the scoring champion. Mikan poured in an average of 28.3 points a game, comfortably ahead of Fulks' 26.0.

The Rochester Royals, with Arnie Risen and Bob Davies, finished a game ahead of the Lakers in the Western Division. But in the playoffs, Minneapolis eliminated Rochester in two straight games and went on to defeat Red Auerbach's Washington Capitols in six games for the BAA title. The Capitols had finished the season six games ahead of the New York Knicks and then eliminated the Knicks, two games to one, in the playoffs.

Old NBL players dominated the All-BAA selections as Mikan and Jim Pollard of Minneapolis and Rochester's Davies, who had led the league in assists and averaged 15.1 points, all made the team. Mikan was a unanimous pick. Joining them were two familiar faces, Fulks, and Max Zaslofsky of Chicago, each making the all-league squad for the third consecutive year.

Fulks turned in the outstanding individual performance of the season by scoring 63 points against the Indianapolis Jets. His outburst totally eclipsed the league's old scoring high of 47 points, set by Carl Braun of New York the season before.

The Lakers played the famed Harlem Globetrotters twice and split the two games. One of the contests attracted a crowd of 20,046. The BAA's Philadelphia Warriors also took a game from the Globetrotters, winning 58-54.

The NBL, breathing its last, added Denver, Dayton, Hammond, and Waterloo to make up for the loss of the four teams that jumped to the BAA and the disbanding of the Toledo and Flint franchises. The Anderson Duffey Packers finished first in the East and defeated the Oshkosh All-Stars, Western champions, in the playoffs. Don Otten of the Tri-Cities Blackhawks topped the NBL's scorers.

Otten, along with Dick Mehen of Waterloo, Al Cervi of Syracuse, Frank Brian of Anderson, and Gene Englund of Oshkosh, made the All-NBL team.

STANDINGS

EASTERN DIVISION

	W.	L.	Pct.
Washington	38	22	.633
New York	32	28	.533
Baltimore	29	31	.483
Philadelphia	28	32	.467
Boston	25	35	.417
Providence	12	48	.200

WESTERN DIVISION

	W.	L.	Pct.
Rochester	45	15	.750
Minneapolis	44	16	.733
Chicago	38	22	.633
St. Louis	29	31	.483
Fort Wayne	22	38	.367
Indianapolis	18	42	.300

PLAYOFFS

FIRST ROUND

Washington defeated Philadelphia 2 games
  to 0
New York defeated Baltimore 2 games to 1
Rochester defeated St. Louis 2 games to 0
Minneapolis defeated Chicago 2 games to 0

SEMIFINALS

Minneapolis defeated Rochester 2 games to 0
Washington defeated New York 2 games to 1

CHAMPIONSHIP

Minneapolis defeated Washington 4 games
  to 2

TOP SCORERS

	Pts.	Ave.
George Mikan, Minneapolis	1698	28.3
Joe Fulks, Philadelphia	1560	26.0
Max Zaslofsky, Chicago	1197	20.6
Arnie Risen, Rochester	995	16.6
Ed Sadowski, Philadelphia	920	15.3

LEADERS IN ASSISTS

	No.	Ave.
Bob Davies, Rochester	321	5.4
Andy Phillip, Chicago	319	5.3
John Logan, St. Louis	276	4.8
Ernie Calverley, Providence	251	4.3
George Senesky, Philadelphia	233	3.9

UPI

Chicago's Andy Phillip, second in NBA in assists, tries to stop New York's Paul Noel.

The war between the leagues came to an end as the BAA and the NBL merged to form the new National Basketball Association. The merger left an unwieldy 17-team league, divided into three divisions.

The Central Division included Minneapolis, Rochester, Fort Wayne, Chicago, and St. Louis — BAA teams the year before. New York, Washington, Philadelphia, Boston, and Philadelphia from the BAA and Syracuse of the NBL were in the Eastern Division. The West contained six former NBL teams, Indianapolis, Anderson, Tri-Cities, Sheboygan, Waterloo, and Denver.

But despite all the new teams and new alignments, the league still had a familiar look as George Mikan and the Minneapolis Lakers won the championship. Mikan set all sorts of individual records, including the highest scoring average, 27.4 points a game; most field goals, 649; and most foul shots, 567 of 728 attempts. He rolled up the highest one-game scoring total of the season with 51 points against Rochester.

Even with Mikan, Jim Pollard, Vern Mikkelsen, Arnie Ferrin, and Slater Martin, the Lakers still had to beat Rochester in a special playoff after the two teams had tied for the Central title.

In the championship round of the playoffs, Minneapolis defeated Anderson, which had surprised Western champion Indianapolis, in two straight games and Syracuse, the Eastern champion, in a hard-fought six-game series.

Two outstanding rookies, Ed Macauley with St. Louis and Alex Groza with Indianapolis, came into the league. Groza, who played his college ball at Kentucky, finished second to Mikan with a 23.4 scoring average and led the NBA in field-goal accuracy with a 47.8 mark. Macauley, a two-time All-American at St. Louis University, was fifth with a 16.1 average. Another rookie, Dick McGuire of the New York Knicks, topped the league in assists.

Mikan came within one vote of being a unanimous all-league pick for the second straight year. Joining him on the team were his teammate Jim Pollard, Max Zaslofsky of Chicago, Bobby Davies of Rochester, and Groza.

The Lakers played the Harlem Globetrotters twice, winning both games. One of the games, in Chicago, attracted a crowd of 21,666.

STANDINGS

EASTERN DIVISION

	W.	L.	Pct.
Syracuse	51	13	.797
New York	40	28	.588
Washington	32	36	.471
Philadelphia	26	42	.382
Baltimore	25	43	.368
Boston	22	46	.324

WESTERN DIVISION

	W.	L.	Pct.
Indianapolis	39	25	.609
Anderson	37	27	.578
Tri-Cities	29	35	.453
Sheboygan	22	40	.355
Waterloo	19	43	.306
Denver	11	51	.177

CENTRAL DIVISION

	W.	L.	Pct.
Minneapolis *	51	17	.750
Rochester	51	17	.750
Fort Wayne *	40	28	.588
Chicago	40	28	.588
St. Louis	26	42	.382

* Won playoff to break tie

PLAYOFFS

FIRST ROUND

Syracuse defeated Philadelphia 2 games to 0
New York defeated Washington 2 games to 0
Minneapolis defeated Chicago 2 games to 0
Fort Wayne defeated Rochester 2 games to 0
Indianapolis defeated Sheboygan 2 games to 1
Anderson defeated Tri-Cities 2 games to 1

SECOND ROUND

Syracuse defeated New York 2 games to 1
Minneapolis defeated Fort Wayne 2 games to 0
Anderson defeated Indianapolis 2 games to 1

THIRD ROUND

Minneapolis defeated Anderson 2 games to 0

CHAMPIONSHIP

Minneapolis defeated Syracuse 4 games to 2

TOP SCORERS

	Pts.	Ave.
George Mikan, Minneapolis	1865	27.4
Alex Groza, Indianapolis	1496	23.4
Frank Brian, Anderson	1138	17.8
Max Zaslofsky, Chicago	1115	16.4
Ed Macauley, St. Louis	1081	16.1

LEADERS IN ASSISTS

	No.	Ave.
Dick McGuire, New York	386	5.7
Andy Phillip, Chicago	377	5.8
Bob Davies, Rochester	294	4.6
George Senesky, Philadelphia	264	3.9
Al Cervi, Syracuse	264	4.7

New York's Sweetwater Clifton, ex-Globetrotter, was one of the first Negroes in the NBA.

UPI

When the Chicago franchise disbanded after the 1949–50 season, the remaining teams divided up the Stags' roster. The Boston Celtics came up with Bob Cousy, a 6-1 guard who many other teams considered too small for the NBA. But this season, and for many seasons to come, Cousy would prove just how wrong were the skeptics. He averaged 15.6 points a game, ninth best in the league, and was named Rookie of the Year.

For the first time Negroes played in the NBA. The New York Knicks obtained Nat "Sweetwater" Clifton from the Harlem Globetrotters, and the Boston Celtics drafted Chuck Cooper of Duquesne. In general, though, rookies had trouble making the teams, with only 12 first-year men in the league.

The NBA got down to a more manageable size when six franchises — Chicago, St. Louis, Anderson, Waterloo, Sheboygan, and Denver — dropped out. The remaining 11 teams were organized into two divisions. The collapse of the Washington Capitols on January 9, though, left the league with 10 teams for most of the season.

The Rochester Royals, with Arnie Risen, Bob Davies, and Bob Wanzer, ended the Minneapolis Lakers' three-year reign as World Champions. The Royals eliminated the Lakers, three games to one, in the playoff semifinals after having finished three games behind Minneapolis in the West. In the East, Philadelphia finished two-and-a-half games ahead of Boston, coached by Red Auerbach, and four games ahead of New York. But the Knicks won the Eastern playoffs before losing to Rochester, four games to three, for the championship.

Two highlights of the campaign were a 19-18 victory by Fort Wayne over Minneapolis in a stalling battle and a 75-73 triumph by Indianapolis over Rochester in six overtimes.

As he had every season since entering the league, George Mikan won the scoring title with a 28.4 average; Alex Groza of the Indianapolis Jets was second with a 21.7 mark; and "Easy Ed" Macauley of Boston was third with 20.4. For the second year in a row Groza was the NBA's most accurate shooter, connecting on 47.0 percent of his shots from the floor. Andy Phillip of Philadelphia led in assists and the Syracuse Nationals' Dolph Schayes topped the NBA in rebounding.

The league played its first All-Star Game in the Boston Garden on March 2 and 10,094 fans turned out to see the East down the West, 111-94. The winners' Macauley, MVP, led the scorers with 20 points and held Mikan to four field goals.

The All-NBA team included Mikan, a unanimous selection; Groza and Macauley, each in his second NBA season; Bob Davies of the champion Rochester Royals; and Ralph Beard of Indianapolis, who had been a college teammate of Groza at Kentucky.

STANDINGS

EASTERN DIVISION

	W.	L.	Pct.
Philadelphia	40	26	.606
Boston	39	30	.565
New York	36	30	.545
Syracuse	32	34	.485
Baltimore	24	42	.364
Washington *	10	25	.286

* Disbanded Jan. 10, 1951

WESTERN DIVISION

	W.	L.	Pct.
Minneapolis	44	24	.647
Rochester	41	27	.603
Fort Wayne	32	36	.471
Indianapolis	31	37	.456
Tri-Cities	25	43	.368

PLAYOFFS

FIRST ROUND

New York defeated Boston 2 games to 0
Syracuse defeated Philadelphia 2 games to 0
Rochester defeated Fort Wayne 2 games to 1
Minneapolis defeated Indianapolis 2 games
    to 1

SEMIFINALS

New York defeated Syracuse 3 games to 2
Rochester defeated Minneapolis 3 games to 1

CHAMPIONSHIP

Rochester defeated New York 4 games to 3

TOP SCORERS

	Pts.	Ave.
George Mikan, Minneapolis	1932	28.4
Alex Groza, Indianapolis	1429	21.7
Ed Macauley, Boston	1384	20.4
Joe Fulks, Philadelphia	1236	18.7
Frank Brian, Tri-Cities	1144	16.8

TOP REBOUNDERS

	No.	Ave.
Dolph Schayes, Syracuse	1080	16.4
George Mikan, Minneapolis	958	14.1
Harry Gallatin, New York	800	12.1
Arnie Risen, Rochester	795	12.0
Alex Groza, Indianapolis	709	10.7

LEADERS IN ASSISTS

	No.	Ave.
Andy Phillip, Philadelphia	414	6.3
Dick McGuire, New York	400	6.3
George Senesky, Philadelphia	342	5.3
Bob Cousy, Boston	341	4.9
Ralph Beard, Indianapolis	318	4.8

Knick's Vince Boryla has Celtic Ed Macauley up in the air.

1951-52

Minneapolis regained the league championship, its second since the merger of the BAA and the NBL. The Lakers did it with big, strong scorers and rebounders in 6-10 George Mikan, 6-8 Vern Mikkelsen, and 6-3 Jim Pollard. The Laker stars weren't hampered by the wider free throw lanes, increased from six to twelve feet, designed to keep pivot men further from the basket by enlarging the three-second area.

For the first time in his NBA career, though, Mikan failed to lead the league in scoring. Instead the honors went to Paul Arizin, a 6-4 forward in his second pro season with the Philadelphia Warriors. Arizin finished with a 25.4 average, and Mikan was second with 23.8. Arizin led the NBA in field-goal accuracy with 44.8 percent, and also hit on 17 successive free throws, the longest streak of the season.

Mikan had the best single game of the year, scoring 61 points against Rochester on January 20. This was only two less than the NBA record set by Joe Fulks. Larry Foust of Fort Wayne and Mel Hutchins of Milwaukee tied for the rebounding lead.

The divisional races were the closest in the NBA's short history. Syracuse won by a single game over New York in the East, and Rochester, the defending NBA champion, by the same margin in the West. Neither of the first-place finishers made it to the playoff finals, however. The Knicks ousted Syracuse and Minneapolis eliminated Rochester. In the playoff finals, the Lakers beat the Knicks in a seven-game series for the title.

The league showed signs of increasing stability, with only one franchise shift. The Tri-Cities Blackhawks, one of the old NBL teams, moved to Milwaukee and became the Milwaukee Hawks. The change of scenery didn't help, though, as the team finished last in the West for the second straight year.

As usual Mikan headed the selections for the All-NBA team. The other members were Arizin; Boston's Bob Cousy, the third-leading scorer with a 21.7 average; Ed Macauley, Cousy's teammate and the NBA's fourth scorer with a 19.2 average; Bob Davies of Rochester, fifth with 16.2; and Dolph Schayes of Syracuse. Davies and Schayes shared the fifth spot on the team.

For the second consecutive year the All-Star Game was held in Boston and for the second time the East scored a convincing victory. Arizin led the East to a 108-91 triumph with 26 points and was named the game's Most Valuable Player. Mikan scored 26 for the West.

STANDINGS

EASTERN DIVISION

	W.	L.	Pct.
Syracuse	40	26	.606
Boston	39	27	.591
New York	37	29	.561
Philadelphia	33	33	.500
Baltimore	20	46	.303

WESTERN DIVISION

	W.	L.	Pct.
Rochester	41	25	.621
Minneapolis	40	26	.606
Indianapolis	34	32	.515
Fort Wayne	29	37	.439
Milwaukee	17	49	.258

PLAYOFFS

FIRST ROUND

Syracuse defeated Philadelphia 2 games to 1
New York defeated Boston 2 games to 1
Minneapolis defeated Indianapolis 2 games to 0
Rochester defeated Fort Wayne 2 games to 0

SEMIFINALS

New York defeated Syracuse 3 games to 1
Minneapolis defeated Rochester 3 games to 1

CHAMPIONSHIP

Minneapolis defeated New York 4 games to 3

TOP SCORERS

	Pts.	Ave.
Paul Arizin, Philadelphia	1674	25.4
George Mikan, Minneapolis	1523	23.8
Bob Cousy, Boston	1433	21.7
Ed Macauley, Boston	1264	19.2
Bob Davies, Rochester	1052	16.2

TOP REBOUNDERS

	No.	Ave.
Mel Hutchins, Milwaukee	880	13.3
Larry Foust, Fort Wayne	880	13.3
George Mikan, Minneapolis	866	13.5
Arnie Risen, Rochester	841	12.7
Dolph Schayes, Syracuse	773	12.3

LEADERS IN ASSISTS

	No.	Ave.
Andy Phillip, Philadelphia	539	8.2
Bob Cousy, Boston	441	6.7
Bob Davies, Rochester	390	6.0
Dick McGuire, New York	388	6.1
Fred Scolari, Baltimore	303	4.7

UPI

Playmaker Bob Cousy showed he could score, with a 50-point game.

Bob Cousy, Boston's incredible guard, turned in the outstanding performance of the year when he scored 50 points against Syracuse in a playoff game on March 21. The game went into four overtimes before the Celtics finally won, 111-105. Cousy made good on 10 of 22 field-goal attempts, most of them from long range, and added a phenomenal 30 of 32 free throws. His 50 points were the most ever scored in a playoff game.

Despite Cousy's heroics, the playoffs had a familiar look as Minneapolis defeated New York for its second straight title and fourth in five seasons. The Knicks battled into the playoff finals for the third straight time and lost for the third consecutive year.

For the first time in its history the NBA opened the season with the same teams that had finished the year before. The Eastern division race was particularly close, with New York finishing half a game ahead of

Syracuse and a game and a half in front of the Celtics. In the West, Minneapolis wound up four games ahead of second-place Rochester.

Neil Johnston, Philadelphia's 6-8 center, won the scoring title with a 22.3 average. The Lakers' George Mikan, with a 20.6 mark, was second. Johnston was also the NBA's most accurate shooter, hitting on 45.2 percent of his shots. Mikan led in rebounds with a 14.4 average.

Seventeen individual and team records fell during the season. Boston's Cousy set new game (18) and season (547) records for assists and also tied the league record by making 15 of 15 free throws in a game.

Bill Sharman, Cousy's backcourt partner on the Celtics, made his first 11 shots from the floor against Philadelphia for a single-game mark. Another Celtic, Ed Macauley, and Mikan each scored 46 points in a game, high for the season. Mikan's performance was in a game against Baltimore in which he scored 32 points in the first half, 19 in the second quarter.

The West won its first All-Star Game in three tries, defeating the East, 79-75, before 10,322 fans in Fort Wayne. Mikan was the leading scorer with 22 points and was chosen MVP, but it was Bobby Davies of Rochester who broke the game open by scoring eight straight points for the West in the final five minutes of play.

Syracuse's Dolph Schayes was named to the All-NBA team with Mikan, Johnston, Cousy, and Macauley.

STANDINGS

EASTERN DIVISION

	W.	L.	Pct.
New York	47	23	.671
Syracuse	47	24	.662
Boston	46	25	.648
Baltimore	16	54	.229
Philadelphia	12	57	.174

WESTERN DIVISION

	W.	L.	Pct.
Minneapolis	48	22	.686
Rochester	44	26	.629
Fort Wayne	36	33	.522
Indianapolis	28	43	.394
Milwaukee	27	44	.380

PLAYOFFS

FIRST ROUND

New York defeated Baltimore 2 games to 0
Boston defeated Syracuse 2 games to 0
Fort Wayne defeated Rochester 2 games to 1
Minneapolis defeated Indianapolis 2 games to 0

SEMIFINALS

New York defeated Boston 3 games to 1
Minneapolis defeated Fort Wayne 3 games to 2

CHAMPIONSHIP

Minneapolis defeated New York 4 games to 1

TOP SCORERS

	Pts.	Ave.
Neil Johnston, Philadelphia	1564	22.3
George Mikan, Minneapolis	1442	20.6
Bob Cousy, Boston	1407	19.8
Ed Macauley, Boston	1402	20.3
Dolph Schayes, Syracuse	1262	17.8

TOP REBOUNDERS

	No.	Ave.
George Mikan, Minneapolis	1007	14.4
Neil Johnston, Philadelphia	976	13.9
Dolph Schayes, Syracuse	920	13.0
Harry Gallatin, New York	916	13.1
Mel Hutchins, Milwaukee	793	11.2

LEADERS IN ASSISTS

	No.	Ave.
Bob Cousy, Boston	547	7.7
Andy Phillip, Fort Wayne	397	5.7
George King, Syracuse	364	5.1
Dick McGuire, New York	296	4.9
Paul Seymour, Syracuse	294	4.4

Warriors' Neil Johnston set a Madison Square Garden pro scoring mark with 50 points.

UPI

1953-54

George Mikan, the magnificent 6-10 center, played his last full season as a pro and led the Minneapolis Lakers to their third straight championship and fifth in six years in three leagues. Mikan, later named the greatest basketball player of the first half of the century in an Associated Pres poll, averaged 18.1 points a game, fourth best in the league. He also was the all-league center, as he was in every year of his pro career.

Indianapolis dropped out of the league, leaving five teams in the East and four in the West. Both divisional races were close, with New York taking the Eastern crown by two games over Syracuse and Boston, and Minneapolis winning by two over Rochester in the West. Syracuse made it to the playoff finals but bowed to Minneapolis in a seven-game series for the championship.

The Philadelphia Warriors' Neil Johnston retained the scoring title with a 24.4 average. Bob Cousy of Boston was second with a 19.2 mark, and his teammate Ed Macauley was third.

Macauley was the NBA's most accurate shooter from the floor with a .486 percentage, and Boston's Bill Sharman was tops from the free-throw line, making 84.4 percent of his shots. New York's Harry "The Horse" Gallatin hauled in a record-setting total of 1,098 rebounds, an average of 15.3 a game. What made his feat more remarkable was that, at 6-6, Gallatin was usually battling against taller men.

The East scored a 98-93 overtime victory in the annual All-Star Game, staged before a crowd of 16,478 in Madison Square Garden. Mikan tied the score at 84-all by hitting two free throws with no time left in regulation play. But Cousy, the game's MVP, scored 10 of the East's 14 points in the overtime period for the East's third victory in four games. Jim Pollard of Minneapolis led the West with 23 points.

The All-NBA team included Cousy, who was a unanimous pick; Johnston, Mikan, Dolph Schayes of Syracuse; and Gallatin. Ray Felix, a skinny 6-11 center from

Long Island University, averaged 17.6 points a game for
Baltimore and won Rookie of the Year honors.

STANDINGS

EASTERN DIVISION

	W.	L.	Pct.
New York	44	28	.611
Boston	42	30	.583
Syracuse	42	30	.583
Philadelphia	29	43	.403
Baltimore	16	56	.222

WESTERN DIVISION

	W.	L.	Pct.
Minneapolis	46	26	.639
Rochester	44	28	.611
Fort Wayne	40	32	.556
Milwaukee	21	51	.292

PLAYOFFS

FIRST ROUND

Boston defeated New York 2 games to 0
Syracuse defeated New York 2 games to 0
Syracuse defeated Boston 2 games to 0
Rochester defeated Fort Wayne 2 games to 0
Minneapolis defeated Fort Wayne 2 games to 0
Minneapolis defeated Rochester 1 game to 0

SEMIFINALS

Syracuse defeated Boston 2 games to 0
Minneapolis defeated Rochester 2 games to 1

CHAMPIONSHIP

Minneapolis defeated Syracuse 4 games to 3

TOP SCORERS

	Pts.	Ave.
Neil Johnston, Philadelphia	1759	24.4
Bob Cousy, Boston	1383	19.2
Ed Macauley, Boston	1344	18.9
George Mikan, Minneapolis	1306	18.1
Ray Felix, Baltimore	1269	17.6

TOP REBOUNDERS

	No.	Ave.
Harry Gallatin, New York	1098	15.3
George Mikan, Minneapolis	1028	14.3
Larry Foust, Fort Wayne	967	13.4
Ray Felix, Baltimore	958	13.3
Dolph Schayes, Syracuse	879	12.1

LEADERS IN ASSISTS

	No.	Ave.
Bob Cousy, Boston	578	7.2
Andy Phillip, Fort Wayne	449	6.3
Paul Seymour, Syracuse	364	5.1
Dick McGuire, New York	354	5.2
Bob Davies, Rochester	323	4.5

UPI

Minneapolis' Jim Pollard captures rebound in face of Ft. Wayne's Paul Walther.

The NBA made several important rules changes in an attempt to speed up play and eliminate excessive fouling. The most important was the introduction of the 24-second rule, requiring a team to shoot within 24 seconds of gaining possession of the ball. The league also decided to limit teams to six personal fouls a quarter. Any additional personals would be punished by a bonus foul shot.

The Syracuse Nationals won the league championship, defeating the Fort Wayne Pistons in the final playoff series. The Nats won the title when George King tossed in a foul shot with ten seconds remaining in the decisive seventh game to break a 91-91 deadlock.

Syracuse had won the Eastern Division title by five games over New York, and Fort Wayne had finished three games ahead of the defending NBA champion,

Minneapolis, in the West. The Lakers, champions in five of the last six seasons, had to get used to playing without George Mikan, their great center who had retired to attend law school.

The Baltimore Bullets disbanded early in the season after having played 14 games and their players were divided among the eight remaining teams.

Neil Johnston of Philadelphia continued his domination as the league's top point-maker, winning the scoring title for the third consecutive year. He averaged 22.7 points a game, beating out teammate Paul Arizin and Bob Cousy of Boston. Johnston also led in rebounding with a 15.1 average. Cousy was the league leader in assists, but Rochester's Bob Davies, playing his last season, set a single-game assist record of 20.

Several other outstanding individual performances highlighted the year. Johnston scored 45 points in a game against Rochester, and grabbed 39 rebounds against Syracuse. Boston's Bill Sharman, the league's best foul shooter, converted a record 50 consecutive free throws over a 10-game stretch.

The season's outstanding rookie was Bob Pettit, Milwaukee's 6-9 forward. Pettit, from Louisiana State, finished fourth in scoring with a 20.4 average. The Hawks also came up with another good rookie in Frank Selvy. Selvy came to Milwaukee after the collapse of the Baltimore franchise and wound up as the NBA's fifth-leading scorer with a 19.0 average. He reached a single-game peak of 42 against Minneapolis.

The East scored a 100–91 victory in the annual All-Star Game, played before 13,138 in Madison Square Garden. The Boston backcourt combination of Cousy and Sharman led the East, with Sharman picked as the game's MVP. He scored 15 points, Cousy 20.

Pettit, Johnston, and Cousy made the All-NBA team, along with Dolph Schayes of Syracuse and Larry Foust of Fort Wayne. Schayes had averaged 18.8 points and 12.3 rebounds in leading the Nationals to the championship and Foust, a 6-9 center, was the NBA's leader in field-goal accuracy with a .487 percentage.

STANDINGS

EASTERN DIVISION

	W.	L.	Pct.
Syracuse	43	29	.597
New York	38	34	.528
Boston	36	36	.500
Philadelphia	33	39	.458

WESTERN DIVISION

	W.	L.	Pct.
Fort Wayne	43	29	.597
Minneapolis	40	32	.556
Rochester	29	43	.403
Milwaukee	29	46	.361

PLAYOFFS

FIRST ROUND

Boston defeated New York 2 games to 1
Minneapolis defeated Rochester 2 games to 1

SEMIFINALS

Syracuse defeated Boston 3 games to 1
Fort Wayne defeated Minneapolis 3 games to 1

CHAMPIONSHIP

Syracuse defeated Fort Wayne 4 games to 3

TOP SCORERS

	Pts.	Ave.
Neil Johnston, Philadelphia	1631	22.7
Paul Arizin, Philadelphia	1512	21.0
Bob Cousy, Boston	1504	21.2
Bob Pettit, Milwaukee	1466	20.4
Frank Selvy, Milwaukee	1348	19.0

TOP REBOUNDERS

	No.	Ave.
Neil Johnston, Philadelphia	1085	15.1
Harry Gallatin, New York	995	13.8
Bob Pettit, Milwaukee	994	13.8
Dolph Schayes, Syracuse	887	12.3
Ray Felix, New York	818	11.4

LEADERS IN ASSISTS

	No.	Ave.
Bob Cousy, Boston	557	7.8
Dick McGuire, New York	542	7.6
Andy Phillip, Fort Wayne	491	7.7
Paul Seymour, Syracuse	483	6.7
Slater Martin, Minneapolis	427	5.9

St. Louis Hawk Bob Pettit (9) was MVP, and a lot else.

Bob Pettit, the NBA's Rookie of the Year a season ago, proved totally immune to the sophomore jinx. The 6-9 forward swept just about all the league's individual honors. He led the league in scoring, with a 25.7 average; in rebounding with a 16.2 average; won the Podoloff Cup as the NBA's Most Valuable Player; and was the outstanding player in the All-Star Game.

But despite Pettit's individual feats for the well-traveled Hawks, now in St. Louis, Philadelphia won the NBA championship, its first since the league's initial season. The Warriors won by six games over Boston in the East and Fort Wayne took the Western title by four games over Minneapolis. Both teams made it to the playoff finals, with Philadelphia defeating Fort Wayne, four games to one. Paul Arizin and Neil Johnston, the NBA's second- and third-leading scorers, led the Warriors to victory.

The Hawks, who had started out as the Tri-Cities Blackhawks in the old NBL, moved from Milwaukee to St. Louis in the only franchise shift of the season. Another link to the past was broken when the Pistons' Max Zaslofsky, who had been on four all-league teams, was waived out of the circuit. This left Connie Simmons of Rochester as the only player who had been in the league since its founding as the Basketball Association of America a decade earlier.

Joe Lapchick, who had coached the New York Knickerbockers for nine seasons, retired in February and was succeeded by Vince Boryla, one of his former players.

The West, behind Pettit's brilliant all-around play, defeated the East, 108-94, in the annual All-Star Game at Rochester. Pettit scored 20 points and grabbed 24 rebounds on his way to MVP honors in the game. Philadelphia's Johnston scored 17 to pace the losers.

The All-NBA team included Pettit, the Warriors' Arizin and Johnston, and Cousy and Bill Sharman of Boston, who were the league's outstanding backcourt duo. Cousy broke his own record with 642 assists during the season and Sharman led the league in foul shooting for the fourth consecutive year with an .867 percentage.

Johnston, with a .457 percentage, was the best shooter from the floor.

The Rochester Royals came up with two outstanding rookies, Maurice Stokes and Jack Twyman. Stokes, the NBA Rookie of the Year from tiny St. Francis of Loretto (Pa.) College, averaged 16.8 points a game and was second to Pettit in rebounding. Twyman averaged 14.4 points a game.

STANDINGS

EASTERN DIVISION

	W.	L.	Pct.
Philadelphia	45	27	.625
Boston	39	33	.542
Syracuse *	35	37	.486
New York	35	37	.486

* Won playoff to break tie

WESTERN DIVISION

	W.	L.	Pct.
Fort Wayne	37	35	.514
Minneapolis *	33	39	.458
St. Louis	33	39	.458
Rochester	31	41	.431

PLAYOFFS

FIRST ROUND

Syracuse defeated Boston 2 games to 1
St. Louis defeated Minneapolis 2 games to 1

SEMIFINALS

Philadelphia defeated Syracuse 3 games to 2
Fort Wayne defeated St. Louis 3 games to 2

CHAMPIONSHIP

Philadelphia defeated Fort Wayne 4 games to 1

TOP SCORERS

	Pts.	Ave.
Bob Pettit, St. Louis	1849	25.7
Paul Arizin, Philadelphia	1741	24.2
Neil Johnston, Philadelphia	1547	22.1
Clyde Lovellette, Minneapolis	1526	21.5
Dolph Schayes, Syracuse	1472	20.4

TOP REBOUNDERS

	No.	Ave.
Bob Pettit, St. Louis	1164	16.2
Maurice Stokes, Rochester	1094	16.3
Clyde Lovellette, Minneapolis	992	14.0
Neil Johnston, Philadelphia	872	12.5
Dolph Schayes, Syracuse	872	12.4

LEADERS IN ASSISTS

	No.	Ave.
Bob Cousy, Boston	642	8.9
Jack George, Philadelphia	457	6.3
Slater Martin, Minneapolis	445	6.2
Andy Phillip, Fort Wayne	410	5.9
George King, Syracuse	410	5.7

UPI

Rookie Bill Russell (6) led ascension of Boston to its first NBA title.

Bill Russell came to the Boston Celtics and brought the key to the NBA championship with him. Russell, a skinny 6-10 rookie from the University of San Francisco, joined the Celtics in December after having led the United States to victory in the 1956 Olympic Games.

With his tremendous rebounding and defensive skills, Russell provided the missing ingredient in the Celtics' championship blend. On offense he made Boston's fast break work, getting the ball to Bob Cousy and Bill Sharman. And on defense his amazing shot-blocking talent intimidated opposing shooters.

Even with Russell, though, the Celtics had to struggle to win their first NBA title. The final playoff series with the St. Louis Hawks went the full seven games. Four of the games were decided by a single basket and two went into double overtime. In the decisive seventh game the lead changed hands 20 times before Frank Ramsey's 20-foot jump shot in the second overtime put Boston ahead, 124-122. The Celts held on to win, 125-123.

Boston won the Eastern title by a comfortable six-game margin over Syracuse, but in the West three teams tied for first. St. Louis, Minneapolis, and Fort Wayne all finished with identical 34-38 marks. In special playoff games to sort out the Western teams, St. Louis beat the Lakers and Pistons.

Paul Arizin of Philadelphia, with a 25.6 average, dethroned St. Louis' Bob Pettit as the scoring champion. Pettit seemed headed for a second straight title until he broke his wrist in mid-February and had to play the rest of the season in a cast. He wound up second with a 24.7 average.

Neil Johnston of Philadelphia, the fourth-leading scorer, was the NBA's most accurate shooter with a .447 percentage from the floor. Bill Sharman, as usual, led in free-throw accuracy. Rochester's Maurice Stokes was the leading rebounder, although Russell, who missed a third of the season because of the Olympics, had the highest rebound average.

The East defeated the West, 109-97, in the All-Star Game at Boston. Cousy won the game's MVP award for the second time with his brilliant floor play and Sharman stunned the crowd with a 70-foot field goal.

Cousy was the NBA's Most Valuable Player and was joined on the All-NBA team by Sharman, Arizin, Dolph Schayes of Syracuse, and Pettit. Another Boston player, Tom Heinsohn, won Rookie of the Year honors, averaging 16.2 points a game.

STANDINGS

EASTERN DIVISION

	W.	L.	Pct.
Boston	44	28	.611
Syracuse	38	34	.528
Philadelphia	37	35	.514
New York	36	36	.500

WESTERN DIVISION

	W.	L.	Pct.
St. Louis *	34	38	.472
Minneapolis	34	38	.472
Fort Wayne	34	38	.472
Rochester	31	41	.431

* Won playoff with Minneapolis and Fort Wayne to break tie

PLAYOFFS

FIRST ROUND

Syracuse defeated Philadelphia 2 games to 0
Minneapolis defeated Fort Wayne 2 games to 0

SEMIFINALS

Boston defeated Syracuse 3 games to 0
St. Louis defeated Minneapolis 3 games to 0

CHAMPIONSHIP

Boston defeated St. Louis 4 games to 3

TOP SCORERS

	Pts.	Ave.
Paul Arizin, Philadelphia	1817	25.6
Bob Pettit, St. Louis	1755	24.7
Dolph Schayes, Syracuse	1617	22.5
Neil Johnston, Philadelphia	1575	22.8
George Yardley, Fort Wayne	1547	21.5

TOP REBOUNDERS

	No.	Ave.
Maurice Stokes, Rochester	1256	17.4
Bob Pettit, St. Louis	1037	14.6
Dolph Schayes, Syracuse	1008	14.0
Bill Russell, Boston	943	19.6
Clyde Lovellette, Minneapolis	932	13.5

LEADERS IN ASSISTS

	No.	Ave.
Bob Cousy, Boston	478	7.4
Jack McMahon, St. Louis	367	5.1
Maurice Stokes, Rochester	331	4.6
Jack George, Philadelphia	307	4.6
Slater Martin, St. Louis	269	4.1

George Yardley was top NBA scorer when Pistons moved to Detroit.

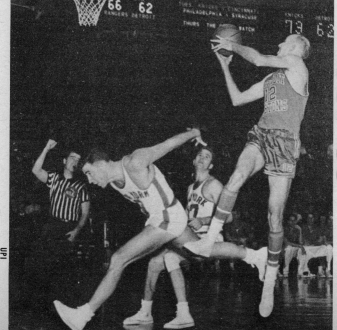

1957-58

UPI

121

The St. Louis Hawks, behind the magnificent shooting of Bob Pettit, dethroned Boston in the playoffs and won their first NBA championship. The Hawks and Celtics met in the playoff finals for the second straight year, with St. Louis winning, four games to two. The Hawks' four triumphs came by a total of eight points.

In the decisive sixth playoff game, Pettit scored 50 points, including 19 of the Hawks' last 21. The Hawks' victory gave the NBA its fifth different champion in five seasons.

Boston won by eight games over Syracuse in the East and St. Louis took the Western crown by the same margin over Detroit. The Celtics' hopes of repeating as league champions, though, were crushed when Bill Russell, their outstanding center, sprained his ankle in the third playoff game against St. Louis and had to miss the remainder of the series.

As part of the NBA's shift away from the smaller cities, the Rochester franchise moved to Cincinnati and the Fort Wayne Pistons relocated in Detroit.

George Yardley of Detroit captured the scoring title with a 27.8 average. His total of 2,001 points was a record, eclipsing the old mark of 1,932 set by George Mikan in the 1951–52 season. Yardley scored more than 50 points in a game twice, getting 51 against Boston on January 15 and topping that with 52 against Syracuse on February 4.

Dolph Schayes of Syracuse was second in scoring with a 24.9 average, followed by Pettit with 24.6. Jack Twyman of Cincinnati led the circuit in field-goal accuracy with a .452 percentage and Schayes, with a .904 percentage, dethroned perennial leader Bill Sharman of Boston as the best free-throw shooter. Russell topped the rebounders with a 22.7 average, and Cousy, averaging 7.1 assists a game, led in that department for the seventh straight season.

Harry Gallatin of Detroit, who played in his 682nd regular season game and 65th consecutive playoff contest, retired after ten years in the NBA.

The Hawks' Cliff Hagan and the Minneapolis Lakers'

Dick Garmaker each scored 26 points in a single quarter, a league record.

In the All-Star Game at St. Louis, Cousy broke the game open with seven consecutive points to lead the East to a 130-118 victory. But Pettit, with 28 points and 26 rebounds, was the MVP.

Bill Russell won the Most Valuable Player award for the season in a vote of the players, but the annual poll of sportswriters only put him on the All-NBA second team. The first team included Schayes, Yardley, Pettit, Cousy, and Sharman. Woody Sauldsberry of Philadelphia was the Rookie of the year.

In a tragic development, Maurice Stokes, the 6-7 Cincinnati forward who had been the 1955–56 Rookie of the Year, was stricken with encephalitis. The crippling brain disease ended his career and put him in the hospital for extensive treatment.

STANDINGS

EASTERN DIVISION

	W.	L.	Pct.
Boston	49	23	.681
Syracuse	41	31	.569
Philadelphia	37	35	.514
New York	35	37	.486

WESTERN DIVISION

	W.	L.	Pct.
St. Louis	41	31	.569
Detroit	33	39	.458
Cincinnati	33	39	.458
Minneapolis	19	53	.264

PLAYOFFS

FIRST ROUND

Philadelphia defeated Syracuse 2 games to 1
Detroit defeated Cincinnati 2 games to 0

SEMIFINALS

Boston defeated Philadelphia 4 games to 1
St. Louis defeated Detroit 4 games to 1

CHAMPIONSHIP

St. Louis defeated Boston 4 games to 2

TOP SCORERS

	Pts.	Ave.
George Yardley, Detroit	2001	27.8
Dolph Schayes, Syracuse	1791	24.9
Bob Pettit, St. Louis	1719	24.6
Clyde Lovellette, Cincinnati	1659	23.4
Paul Arizin, Philadelphia	1406	20.7

TOP REBOUNDERS

	No.	Ave.
Bill Russell, Boston	1564	22.7
Bob Pettit, St. Louis	1216	17.4
Maurice Stokes, Cincinnati	1142	18.1
Dolph Schayes, Syracuse	1022	14.2
John Kerr, Syracuse	963	13.4

LEADERS IN ASSISTS

	No.	Ave.
Bob Cousy, Boston	463	7.1
Dick McGuire, Detroit	454	6.6
Maurice Stokes, Cincinnati	403	6.4
Carl Braun, New York	393	5.5
George King, Cincinnati	337	5.3

UPI

Detroit's Dick McGuire battles Boston's Bill Sharman.

Elgin Baylor, a 6-5 forward from Seattle University, made his pro debut with the Minneapolis Lakers and immediately became one of the NBA's brightest stars. He finished fourth in the individual scoring race with a 24.9 average and became only the third rookie in the history of the league to make the All-NBA team.

Alex Groza in 1949–50 and Bob Pettit in 1954–55 were the others to make the all-league squad in their first seasons.

Baylor boasted tremendous body control, some of the best inside moves ever seen in the league and an amazing capacity for seemingly hanging suspended in midair. His best scoring effort came against Cincinnati on February 25, when he tallied 55 points.

But it was Boston, with Bill Russell in the middle and Bob Cousy and Bill Sharman in backcourt, which won the NBA title, its second in three years. The Celtics coasted to a 12-game spread over New York in the East, Boston's 52 victories setting an NBA record. St. Louis, defending NBA champion, finished 16 games in front of Minneapolis in the West. But the Lakers, led by Baylor, eliminated the Hawks, four games to two in the playoffs.

In the playoff finals Boston scored an unprecedented four-game sweep over the Lakers.

Financially, the league had its best season. Despite the runaways in the two divisional races, attendance reached an all-time high of over 1,449,000. The Knicks drew 18,376 fans in Madison Square Garden on December 25, and bettered that with a crowd of 18,496 on February 3. These were the two largest crowds in the history of the NBA.

Several individual records were set as well. The St. Louis Hawks' Bob Pettit won the scoring crown with a 29.2 average, the highest ever. His total of 2,105 points was also a new mark. Russell set a new standard with 1,612 rebounds for a 23.0 average. Cousy set a new record of 28 assists in a game against Minneapolis, with 19 in one half and 12 in one quarter. The Celtics set a scoring record in that game, bombing the Lakers, 173-139.

Kenny Sears of New York was the most accurate shooter with a .490 percentage from the floor and Sharman recaptured the foul-shooting title from Dolph Schayes with a phenomenal 92.9 percent. Cousy led in assists for the eighth straight year.

The West upset the East, 124-108, in the All-Star Game at Detroit. Elgin Baylor had 24 points and Bob Pettit 25 for the winners. The two were named cowinners of the MVP award.

Neil Johnston and Paul Arizin of Philadelphia, Sharman and Vern Mikkleson of Minneapolis all pushed their career scoring totals above 10,000 points during the season.

Pettit, the league's Most Valuable Player, headed the selections for the All-NBA team. He set a record by scoring over 50 points three times during the year. Joining him on the team were Baylor of the Lakers and Cousy, Sharman, and Russell, the three leaders of the Celtics. Baylor, of course, won Rookie of the Year honors. But another rookie, Hal Greer of Syracuse, put on a phenomenal shooting exhibition by scoring 39 points in the first half, including 18 field goals, against

Boston on February 14. He finished the game with 45 points.

STANDINGS

EASTERN DIVISION

	W.	L.	Pct.
Boston	52	20	.722
New York	40	32	.556
Syracuse	35	37	.486
Philadelphia	32	40	.444

WESTERN DIVISION

	W.	L.	Pct.
St. Louis	49	23	.681
Minneapolis	33	39	.458
Detroit	28	44	.389
Cincinnati	19	53	.264

PLAYOFFS

FIRST ROUND

Syracuse defeated New York 2 games to 0
Minneapolis defeated Detroit 2 games to 1

SEMIFINALS

Boston defeated Syracuse 4 games to 3
Minneapolis defeated St. Louis 4 games to 2

CHAMPIONSHIP

Boston defeated Minneapolis 4 games to 0

TOP SCORERS

	Pts.	Ave.
Bob Pettit, St. Louis	2105	29.2
Jack Twyman, Cincinnati	1857	25.8
Paul Arizin, Philadelphia	1851	26.4
Elgin Baylor, Minneapolis	1742	24.9
Cliff Hagan, St. Louis	1707	23.7

TOP REBOUNDERS

	No.	Ave.
Bill Russell, Boston	1612	23.0
Bob Pettit, St. Louis	1182	16.4
Elgin Baylor, Minneapolis	1050	15.0
John Kerr, Syracuse	1008	13.4
Dolph Schayes, Syracuse	962	13.4

LEADERS IN ASSISTS

	No.	Ave.
Bob Cousy, Boston	557	8.6
Dick McGuire, Detroit	443	6.2
Larry Costello, Syracuse	379	5.4
Richie Guerin, New York	364	5.1
Carl Braun, New York	349	4.8

It's Philadelphia's Chamberlain over Boston's Russell, but Celtics won the title again.

Wilt Chamberlain, the 7-1 center who had played two seasons of college basketball at Kansas and then toured for a year with the Harlem Globetrotters, signed with the Philadelphia Warriors. The Big Dipper had an unparalleled rookie season and quickly proved that he was the greatest offensive force in the league.

The Warrior star set numerous records, including most points, 2,707; highest scoring average, 37.6; most field goals attempted, 2,311; most field goals scored, 1,065; most rebounds, 1,941; highest rebound average, 26.9; and most games with 50 or more points, five.

But Wilt wasn't the only NBA performer to set records. Elgin Baylor, in his second season with Minneapolis, scored 64 points against Boston on November 8, breaking Joe Fulks' 11-year-old record of 63 points. Boston's Bill Russell set a record with 51 rebounds against Syracuse, and Dolph Schayes of Syracuse became the first player to score more than 15,000 points in his career. He finished the season with 15,798 points to move past George Mikan as the all-time scoring leader.

Boston became the first team in six seasons to repeat as league champion. The Celtics edged St. Louis, four games to three, in the playoff finals. Despite the scoring feats of Philadelphia's Chamberlain, Boston had won the Eastern title by 10 games over the second-place Warriors. Boston won 59 games, the most in the NBA's history, and tied a league record with 17 consecutive victories. In the West, St. Louis had an even easier time, breezing to a 16-game margin over the Detroit Pistons.

In the scoring race Cincinnati's Jack Twyman averaged 31.2 points a game. Although no other player had ever averaged over 30 points, Twyman's feat was completely overshadowed by Chamberlain's domination of the scoring statistics.

The Knicks' Kenny Sears led the league in field-goal accuracy with a .477 percentage and Schayes regained the free-throw title from Boston's Bill Sharman with an .892 percentage. The Celtics' Bob Cousy continued as the NBA's top playmaker, setting a season record with

715 assists and becoming the first to get more than 5,000 assists in his career.

The East trounced the West, 125-115, in the All-Star Game at Philadelphia, with Chamberlain scoring 23 points and winning the MVP award. Twyman had 26 for the West.

Chamberlain, the Rookie and Most Valuable Player of the Year headed the All-NBA team. He was joined by Baylor, Cousy, Gene Shue of Detroit, and Bob Pettit of St. Louis. Pettit, along with New York's Carl Braun and St. Louis' Larry Foust, went over the 10,000-point mark for his career.

STANDINGS

EASTERN DIVISION

	W.	L.	Pct.
Boston	59	16	.787
Philadelphia	49	26	.653
Syracuse	45	30	.600
New York	27	48	.360

WESTERN DIVISION

	W.	L.	Pct.
St. Louis	46	29	.613
Detroit	30	45	.400
Minneapolis	25	50	.333
Cincinnati	19	56	.253

PLAYOFFS

FIRST ROUND

Philadelphia defeated Syracuse 2 games to 1
Minneapolis defeated Detroit 2 games to 0

SEMIFINALS

Boston defeated Philadelphia 4 games to 2
St. Louis defeated Minneapolis 4 games to 3

CHAMPIONSHIP

Boston defeated St. Louis 4 games to 3

TOP SCORERS

	Pts.	Ave.
Wilt Chamberlain, Philadelphia	2707	37.6
Jack Twyman, Cincinnati	2338	31.2
Elgin Baylor, Minneapolis	2074	29.6
Bob Pettit, St. Louis	1882	26.1
Cliff Hagan, St. Louis	1858	24.8

TOP REBOUNDERS

	No.	Ave.
Wilt Chamberlain, Philadelphia	1941	26.9
Bill Russell, Boston	1778	24.0
Bob Pettit, St. Louis	1221	16.9
Elgin Baylor, Minneapolis	1150	16.4
Dolph Schayes, Syracuse	959	12.8

LEADERS IN ASSISTS

	No.	Ave.
Bob Cousy, Boston	715	9.5
Guy Rodgers, Philadelphia	482	7.1
Richie Guerin, New York	468	6.3
Larry Costello, Syracuse	446	6.3
Tom Gola, Philadelphia	409	5.4

MALCOLM EMMONS

Rookie Oscar Robertson of Cincinnati keeps Boston's K. C. Jones at arm's length.

The NBA became truly a national league when the Minneapolis Lakers moved to Los Angeles and brought professional basketball to the West Coast. The Lakers came up with an outstanding rookie, Jerry West of West Virginia University, to team with Elgin Baylor, their All-NBA forward.

But the most exciting rookie of the year was Oscar Robertson of the Cincinnati Royals. Robertson had led the nation in scoring for three years as a collegian at Cincinnati and quickly showed that he could score with equal ease in the pro game. The Big O averaged 30.5 points a game, third-best in the NBA, to become the highest-scoring guard in the league's history. Robertson excelled as a playmaker as well, taking over from Boston's Bob Cousy as the leader in assists. Robertson averaged 9.7 assists, the highest in history, and attendance in Cincinnati more than tripled.

Philadelphia's Wilt Chamberlain, who had set a basket of new scoring and rebounding records as a rookie, broke all of his own marks in his second season. He averaged 38.4 points a game and became the first player to score more than 3,000 points in a season, finishing with 3,033. He also set a record for rebounds with an average of 27.2 a game and led in field goal accuracy with a .505 percentage.

The Lakers' sensational Baylor erased his own NBA record by scoring 71 points against New York on November 15. He hit on 28 of 48 attempts and 15 of 19 free throws. In addition he grabbed 25 rebounds. Chamberlain produced the most impressive rebounding feat, though, hauling down a record 55 against Boston. Bill Sharman of Boston recaptured the free-throw title with a .921 percentage.

The Celtics established themselves as one of the finest teams in history by winning their third consecutive championship and fourth in five seasons. Boston won the Eastern title with ease, finishing 11 games ahead of the Chamberlain-led Philadelphia Warriors. St. Louis beat the Lakers by 15 games in the West. Boston crushed the Hawks, four games to one, in the playoff finals.

The West bombed the East, 153-131, in the All-Star Game at Syracuse. Bob Pettit of St. Louis posted 29 points for the West, but Oscar Robertson won the MVP award. The Big O had 23 points and 14 assists for the winners.

Bill Russell of Boston won his second Podoloff Cup as the NBA's Most Valuable Player in a vote of the players. But the sportswriters relegated him to the second All-NBA team in their poll. The All-NBA team included Pettit, Chamberlain, Baylor, Cousy, and Robertson, the Rookie of the Year.

New York had the rather dubious distinction of losing a game by 62 points, the greatest margin of defeat in the league's history. The Knicks, who finished last in the East, absorbed a 162-100 beating at the hands of Syracuse on Christmas Day.

STANDINGS

EASTERN DIVISION

	W.	L.	Pct.
Boston	57	22	.722
Philadelphia	46	33	.582
Syracuse	38	41	.481
New York	21	58	.266

WESTERN DIVISION

	W.	L.	Pct.
St. Louis	51	28	.646
Los Angeles	36	43	.456
Detroit	34	45	.430
Cincinnati	33	46	.418

PLAYOFFS

FIRST ROUND

Syracuse defeated Philadelphia 3 games to 0
Los Angeles defeated Detroit 3 games to 2

SEMIFINALS

Boston defeated Syracuse 4 games to 1
St. Louis defeated Los Angeles 4 games to 3

CHAMPIONSHIP

Boston defeated St. Louis 4 games to 1

TOP SCORERS

	Pts.	Ave.
Wilt Chamberlain, Philadelphia	3033	38.4
Elgin Baylor, Los Angeles	2538	34.8
Oscar Robertson, Cincinnati	2165	30.5
Bob Pettit, St. Louis	2120	27.9
Jack Twyman, Cincinnati	1997	25.3

TOP REBOUNDERS

	No.	Ave.
Wilt Chamberlain, Philadelphia	2149	27.2
Bob Pettit, St. Louis	1540	20.3
Elgin Baylor, Los Angeles	1447	19.8
Bailey Howell, Detroit	1111	14.4
Willie Naulls, New York	1055	13.4

LEADERS IN ASSISTS

	No.	Ave.
Oscar Robertson, Cincinnati	690	9.7
Guy Rodgers, Philadelphia	677	8.9
Bob Cousy, Boston	591	7.8
Gene Shue, Detroit	530	6.8
Richie Guerin, New York	503	6.4

Bob Cousy, a 15,000-point man, shoots against Royals' Arlen Bockhorn and Oscar Robertson.

MALCOLM EMMONS

1961-62

Wilt Chamberlain, Philadelphia's mighty 7-1 center, dwarfed all past scoring feats by recording 100 points in a single game. Wilt's incredible performance came in the Warriors' 169-147 victory over New York in Hershey, Pennsylvania, on March 2. The 316 points the two teams scored also set an NBA record.

Chamberlain hit on 36 of 63 field-goal attempts and belied his reputation as the NBA's worst foul shooter by connecting on 28 of 32 shots from the free-throw line.

Wilt again obliterated all season scoring records. He averaged a phenomenal 50.4 points a game, nearly 19 points ahead of Chicago's Walt Bellamy, his nearest rival. In the 80 regular season games, Wilt scored 60 or more points 15 times and over 50 points 44 times. Los Angeles' Elgin Baylor and Jerry West each had 63-point games and Baylor also scored 61 points.

But all this scoring couldn't stop Boston, with a beautifully balanced attack and Bill Russell at center, from winning its fourth consecutive title and fifth in six seasons. The Celtics again made a shambles of the Eastern Division race, finishing 11 games ahead of Philadelphia. Tommy Heinsohn, Boston's best scorer, was no better than 11th in the league with a 22.3 average.

The NBA added a ninth team, the Chicago Packers, which joined the West and finished last. The division winner, Los Angeles, beat Cincinnati by 11 games as St. Louis, Western champions since 1957, dropped to fourth place. The final playoff series between the Lakers and Celtics went the full seven games, with Boston's Sam Jones scoring the winning basket with two seconds left in the deciding game.

Chamberlain won the rebounding title with a 25.6 average. Bellamy, a 6-11 rookie center from Indiana, was the most accurate shooter from the floor with a .513 percentage and Dolph Schayes of Syracuse was tops from the free-throw line with an .896 mark. Cincinnati's Oscar Robertson set a new record, averaging 11.4 assists a game. But Boston's Bob Cousy, who dropped to third in assists, became the first player to go over the 6,000 mark for his career.

Schayes broke Harry Gallatin's consecutive-game record of 682 but saw his own streak snapped at 706 when he suffered a fractured cheekbone on December 26.

Cousy, Bob Pettit of St. Louis, and Paul Arizin of Philadelphia all passed the 15,000-point plateau for their careers.

The West scored a convincing 150-130 victory in the All-Star Game at St. Louis as Bob Pettit, with 27 rebounds and 25 points, took MVP honors for the third time. Wilt Chamberlain set an All-Star scoring record with 42 points for the losers.

Russell, the hub of the Celtics, won his second consecutive Most Valuable Player award but again did not make the All-NBA first team. The All-NBA team included Pettit, Baylor, Chamberlain, West and Robertson, with Chicago's Bellamy the Rookie of the Year.

STANDINGS

EASTERN DIVISION

	W.	L.	Pct.
Boston	60	20	.750
Philadelphia	49	31	.613
Syracuse	41	39	.513
New York	29	51	.363

WESTERN DIVISION

	W.	L.	Pct.
Los Angeles	54	26	.675
Cincinnati	43	37	.538
Detroit	37	43	.463
St. Louis	29	51	.363
Chicago	18	62	.225

PLAYOFFS

FIRST ROUND

Philadelphia defeated Syracuse 3 games to 2
Detroit defeated Cincinnati 3 games to 1

SEMIFINALS

Boston defeated Philadelphia 4 games to 3
Los Angeles defeated Detroit 4 games to 2

CHAMPIONSHIP

Boston defeated Los Angeles 4 games to 3

TOP SCORERS

	Pts.	Ave.
Wilt Chamberlain, Philadelphia	4029	50.4
Walt Bellamy, Chicago	2495	31.6
Oscar Robertson, Cincinnati	2432	30.3
Bob Pettit, St. Louis	2429	31.1
Jerry West, Los Angeles	2310	30.8

TOP REBOUNDERS

	No.	Ave.
Wilt Chamberlain, Philadelphia	2052	25.6
Bill Russell, Boston	1891	24.9
Walt Bellamy, Chicago	1500	19.0
Bob Pettit, St. Louis	1457	18.7
John Kerr, Syracuse	1176	14.7

LEADERS IN ASSISTS

	No.	Ave.
Oscar Robertson, Cincinnati	899	11.4
Guy Rodgers, Philadelphia	663	7.9
Bob Cousy, Boston	584	7.8
Richie Guerin, New York	539	6.9
Gene Shue, Detroit	465	5.8

Western champions Elgin Baylor, left, and Jerry West with Laker coach Fred Schaus.

The NBA continued its march to the West as Eddie Gottlieb, a pioneer professional owner and former coach, sold the Philadelphia Warriors to a San Francisco group. Gottlieb, who was frequently said to have carried his office around in his hat, reportedly received $850,000 for the Warriors.

The Boston Celtics won their fifth consecutive title and sixth in seven years behind their incomparable team of Bob Cousy and Bill Russell. Cousy, generally regarded as the greatest guard in the history of the game, announced his retirement after 13 seasons. The only player to appear in all 13 All-Star Games, Cousy made the All-NBA first team 10 times and the second team twice.

Russell, the league's top defensive player, won his

139

third straight Most Valuable Player award and returned to the All-NBA team after a two-year absence.

As usual, Boston made a runaway of the Eastern Division race. The Celts finished 10 games ahead of Syracuse. In the West, Los Angeles, with Elgin Baylor and Jerry West, successfully defended its divisional title, finishing five games ahead of St. Louis. Both division champions made it into the playoff finals, where Boston defeated the Lakers, four games to two.

San Francisco's Wilt Chamberlain won his fourth scoring title in four seasons in the NBA with a 44.8 average. Baylor finished second with a 34.0 average and Cincinnati's Oscar Robertson was third with 28.3. Chamberlain also led in rebounding with a 24.3 average and in field-goal accuracy, making 52.8 percent of his shots. San Francisco's Guy Rodgers led the league with 10.8 assists a game, most of them coming on passes to Chamberlain. Larry Costello of Syracuse was tops in free-throw accuracy with an .881 percentage.

Syracuse's Dolph Schayes, in his 15th professional season, played in his 1,000th game and scored his 19,000th point during the year. Bob Pettit of St. Louis broke the 17,000 barrier, and Richie Guerin of New York, Cliff Hagan of St. Louis, Tom Heinsohn of Boston, Chamberlain, and Baylor all went over 10,000 points for their careers. Russell, who finished second to Chamberlain in rebounding, became the all-time rebound leader with 11,499.

The East won the All-Star Game at Los Angeles, 115-108, with Robertson scoring 21 points for the East and Pettit 25 for the West. But Russell, who dominated the backboards, won the game MVP award for the second consecutive year.

Baylor, Pettit, Robertson, Russell, and West made the All-NBA team as Chamberlain was relegated to the second team for the first time in his career. Terry Dischinger, who three years before had played on the U.S. Olympic team as a college sophomore, won Rookie of the Year honors with Chicago. He averaged 25.5 points a game.

STANDINGS

EASTERN DIVISION

	W.	L.	Pct.
Boston	58	22	.725
Syracuse	48	32	.600
Cincinnati	42	38	.525
New York	21	59	.263

WESTERN DIVISION

	W.	L.	Pct.
Los Angeles	53	27	.663
St. Louis	48	32	.600
Detroit	34	46	.425
San Francisco	31	49	.388
Chicago	25	55	.313

PLAYOFFS

FIRST ROUND

Cincinnati defeated Syracuse 3 games to 2
St. Louis defeated Detroit 3 games to 1

SEMIFINALS

Boston defeated Cincinnati 4 games to 3
Los Angeles defeated St. Louis 4 games to 3

CHAMPIONSHIP

Boston defeated Los Angeles 4 games to 2

TOP SCORERS

	Pts.	Ave.
Wilt Chamberlain, San Francisco	3586	44.8
Elgin Baylor, Los Angeles	2719	34.0
Oscar Robertson, Cincinnati	2264	28.3
Bob Pettit, St. Louis	2241	28.4
Walt Bellamy, Chicago	2233	27.9

TOP REBOUNDERS

	No.	Ave.
Wilt Chamberlain, San Francisco	1946	24.3
Bill Russell, Boston	1843	23.6
Walt Bellamy, Chicago	1310	16.4
Bob Pettit, St. Louis	1195	15.1
Elgin Baylor, Los Angeles	1146	14.3

LEADERS IN ASSISTS

	No.	Ave.
Guy Rodgers, San Francisco	825	10.6
Oscar Robertson, Cincinnati	758	9.5
Bob Cousy, Boston	515	6.8
Sihugo Green, Chicago	422	5.8
Elgin Baylor, Los Angeles	386	4.8

Philadelphia's Johnny Kerr played in his 745th straight game.

PHILADELPHIA 76ERS

The Boston Celtics, playing without Bob Cousy who had retired to coach at Boston College, won their sixth consecutive NBA title and seventh in eight seasons. The Celtics dynasty, which began when Bill Russell joined the team in 1956–57, reached a new peak in the history of American sports.

The New York Yankees in baseball and the Montreal Canadiens in hockey had each won championships in five straight years, but never before had any major-league professional team won six consecutive titles.

Both divisional races were close. Boston won by five games over Cincinnati, which had Oscar Robertson and rookie sensation Jerry Lucas, and San Francisco, coached by Alex Hannum, held off St. Louis by two games in the West. The Celtics blasted San Francisco, four games to one, in the final playoff series.

Maurice Podoloff, who had served as president of the NBA since its founding 17 years before, retired at the close of the previous season. He was succeeded by Walter Kennedy, the original publicist of the NBA and a former mayor of Stamford, Connecticut. Financially the NBA enjoyed its best season, as attendance climbed above 2,000,000 for the first time. The Chicago franchise, after finishing last in the West for its two seasons of existence, moved to Baltimore. The team revived the nickname of Bullets, which had been used by an earlier Baltimore franchise in the league, and escaped the cellar with a fourth-place finish.

Bob Pettit of St. Louis closed the season with 19,756 career points, making him the most productive scorer ever in the NBA. Dolph Schayes, the first man to score more than 19,000 points, had retired to coach the Philadelphia 76ers. The 76ers, actually the transplanted Syracuse Nationals, brought professional basketball back to Philadelphia after a two-year absence.

Philadelphia's Johnny Kerr played in his 745th consecutive regular season game and 62nd straight playoff contest. Kerr's 707th game in a row broke Schayes' record. An early-season eye injury halted Cincinnati's Jack Twyman's consecutive-game streak at 609.

Wilt Chamberlain won his fifth straight scoring title with a 36.5 average and scored 59 points three times during the year. Oscar Robertson of Cincinnati was second. Robertson also led the league in assists and free-throw accuracy. Cincinnati's Lucas, the Rookie of the Year, beat out Chamberlain as the leader in field-goal accuracy with a .527 percentage and Boston's Russell took the rebounding title.

In the All-Star Game at Boston, Robertson led the East to a 111-107 triumph. The Big O, the MVP both in the game and for the season, scored 26 points. Robertson was a unanimous choice for the All-NBA team, and was joined by Pettit, Chamberlain, and Elgin Baylor, and Jerry West of the Lakers.

After the season, the State Department sponsored an NBA All-Star team on a tour of Europe and the Middle East. The NBA stars swept all 21 games against teams in Poland, Rumania, Yugoslavia, and Egypt.

Cincinnati's Jerry Lucas was Rookie of the Year.

MALCOLM EMMONS

STANDINGS

EASTERN DIVISION

	W.	L.	Pct.
Boston	59	21	.738
Cincinnati	55	25	.688
Philadelphia	34	46	.425
New York	22	58	.275

WESTERN DIVISION

	W.	L.	Pct.
San Francisco	48	32	.600
St. Louis	46	34	.575
Los Angeles	42	38	.525
Baltimore	31	49	.388
Detroit	23	57	.288

PLAYOFFS

FIRST ROUND

Cincinnati defeated Philadelphia 3 games to 2
St. Louis defeated Los Angeles 3 games to 2

SEMIFINALS

Boston defeated Cincinnati 4 games to 1
San Francisco defeated St. Louis 4 games to 3

CHAMPIONSHIP

Boston defeated San Francisco 4 games to 1

TOP SCORERS

	Pts.	Ave.
Wilt Chamberlain, San Francisco	2948	36.5
Oscar Robertson, Cincinnati	2480	31.4
Bob Pettit, St. Louis	2190	27.4
Walt Bellamy, Baltimore	2159	27.0
Jerry West, Los Angeles	2064	27.0

TOP REBOUNDERS

	No.	Ave.
Bill Russell, Boston	1930	24.7
Wilt Chamberlain, San Francisco	1687	21.1
Jerry Lucas, Cincinnati	1375	17.4
Walt Bellamy, Baltimore	1361	17.0
Bob Pettit, St. Louis	1224	15.3

LEADERS IN ASSISTS

	No.	Ave.
Oscar Robertson, Cincinnati	868	11.0
Guy Rodgers, San Francisco	556	7.0
K. C. Jones, Boston	407	5.1
Jerry West, Los Angeles	403	5.6
Wilt Chamberlain, San Francisco	403	5.0

Detroit player-coach Dave DeBusschere goes against Boston's Bill Russell.

1964-65

DETROIT PISTONS

146

News of basketball's biggest trade rocked the NBA world on January 15, the night of the annual All-Star Game in St. Louis. At a postmidnight press conference, San Francisco owner Franklin Mieuli announced that he had traded Wilt Chamberlain, his 7-1 scoring machine, to the Philadelphia 76ers. In return the Warriors received three journeyman players, Connie Dierking, Paul Neuman, and Lee Shaffer, and an undisclosed amount of cash.

Neither the change in locale nor the change to a wider free throw lane (16 feet instead of 12) prevented Wilt from winning his sixth consecutive scoring title with a 34.7 average. Los Angeles' Jerry West was second with 31.0, and Cincinnati's Oscar Robertson was third with 30.4.

The seemingly invincible Boston Celtics won their seventh NBA title in a row and eighth in nine seasons. The Celtics, who won a record 62 games, finished 14 games ahead of Cincinnati in the East. Along the way, the Celtics posted winning streaks of 11 and 16 games.

But it was Philadelphia, which had acquired Wilt in mid-season and finished third in the East, which gave Boston the greatest trouble. The 76ers extended Boston to the full seven games in the Eastern playoff finals. In the decisive final game, Boston's John Havlicek intercepted an in-bounds pass under the Philadelphia basket with five seconds remaining to preserve Boston's 110-109 victory.

The final playoff series came as something of an anticlimax, with Boston whipping Western champion Los Angeles in five games. The Lakers had won in the West by four games over St. Louis. Los Angeles' brilliant Elgin Baylor injured his ankle in the opening game of the Western playoff finals against Baltimore and missed the remainder of the playoffs. Even the fantastic play of the Lakers' Jerry West, who averaged 40.6 points a game during the playoffs, could not overcome Boston's balanced attack.

The Detroit Pistons made NBA history by naming Dave DeBusschere, their outstanding 24-year-old forward, as player-coach. He became the youngest coach in league annals. St. Louis also selected veteran guard Richie Guerin as player-coach.

Chamberlain led the league in field-goal accuracy with a .510 percentage and his Philadelphia teammate, Larry Costello, led in free-throw accuracy with an .877 mark. The Big O was the top playmaker, averaging a record-shattering 11.5 assists a game, and Boston's Bill Russell was the top rebounder.

The East scored a 124-123 victory in the All-Star Game at St. Louis. Robertson scored 28 for the East and Gus Johnson of Baltimore had 25 for the West, but Cincinnati's Jerry Lucas won the MVP award for his outstanding rebounding and 25 points.

Bob Pettit of St. Louis, the most prolific scorer in NBA history, passed the 20,000-point mark for his career and later announced his retirement. Cincinnati's Jack Twyman went over the 15,000 mark and Robertson, Russell, and Los Angeles' Willie Naulls all topped 10,000 career points.

Russell, the NBA's MVP for the fifth time, Baylor, West, Lucas, and Robertson made the All-NBA team. New York's Willis Reed was Rookie of the Year.

Walter Brown, the owner of the Boston Celtics, one of the founders of the NBA and the originator of the All-Star Game, died shortly before the start of the season. The Celtics wore a black strip of cloth on their uniforms in his memory throughout the campaign.

STANDINGS

EASTERN DIVISION

	W.	L.	Pct.
Boston	62	18	.715
Cincinnati	48	32	.600
Philadelphia	40	40	.500
New York	31	49	.388

WESTERN DIVISION

	W.	L.	Pct.
Los Angeles	49	31	.613
St. Louis	45	35	.563
Baltimore	37	43	.463
Detroit	31	49	.388
San Francisco	17	63	.213

PLAYOFFS

FIRST ROUND

Philadelphia defeated Cincinnati 3 games to 1
Baltimore defeated St. Louis 3 games to 1

SEMIFINALS

Boston defeated Philadelphia 4 games to 3
Los Angeles defeated Baltimore 4 games to 2

CHAMPIONSHIP

Boston defeated Los Angeles 4 games to 1

TOP SCORERS

	Pts.	Ave.
Wilt Chamberlain, San Francisco–Philadelphia	2534	34.7
Jerry West, Los Angeles	2292	31.0
Oscar Robertson, Cincinnati	2279	30.4
Sam Jones, Boston	2070	25.9
Elgin Baylor, Los Angeles	2009	27.1

TOP REBOUNDERS

	No.	Ave.
Bill Russell, Boston	1879	24.1
Wilt Chamberlain, San Francisco–Philadelphia	1673	22.9
Nate Thurmond, San Francisco	1395	18.1
Jerry Lucas, Cincinnati	1321	20.0
Willis Reed, New York	1175	14.7

LEADERS IN ASSISTS

	No.	Ave.
Oscar Robertson, Cincinnati	861	11.5
Guy Rodgers, San Francisco	565	7.3
K. C. Jones, Boston	437	5.6
Len Wilkens, St. Louis	431	5.5
Bill Russell, Boston	410	5.3

San Francisco's Rick Barry (24) scored more than 2,000 points in his rookie season.

1965-66

MALCOLM EMMONS

For the first time in a decade, Boston failed to win the Eastern Division title. But the Celtics came back in the playoffs to win their eighth consecutive title and ninth in ten seasons.

The Philadelphia 76ers, with Wilt Chamberlain, Hal Greer, and Chet Walker, won their last 11 games to finish a game ahead of Boston. But Boston easily ousted Philadelphia, four games to one in the Eastern play-off finals.

Los Angeles, with Elgin Baylor and Jerry West, won by seven games over Baltimore in the West and was the only team in the division to win more than half its games. In the playoff finals, Boston, despite the retirement of Tom Heinsohn, the high-scoring forward, beat the Lakers, four games to two.

Chamberlain won his seventh consecutive scoring title with a 33.5 average and also passed Bob Pettit as the all-time high scorer with a career total of 21,486 points in his seven NBA seasons. In addition, Wilt led in field-goal accuracy with a .540 percentage and rebounding with a 24.6 average. Chamberlain also won the Podoloff Cup as the league's Most Valuable Player and continued his streak of never having fouled out in his seven pro seasons.

San Francisco's Rick Barry, a 6-7 rookie from Miami (Fla.), was the season's outstanding rookie. He averaged 25.7 points, fourth best in the league, and reached a single-game high of 57 against New York. Barry joined Chamberlain, New York's Walt Bellamy, and Cincinnati's Oscar Robertson as the only players to score more than 2,000 points in their first seasons.

Robertson retained his playmaking title with an average of 11.1 assists a game, and Boston's Larry Siegfried was the leading foul shooter with an .881 percentage.

Several all-time stars played their last season. They included Cincinnati's Jack Twyman, New York's Tom Gola, Los Angeles' Willie Naulls and Baltimore's John Kerr. Kerr had played in 844 consecutive games since entering the NBA in 1954 until an injury snapped his streak on November 5.

The East won its 11th All-Star Game in 16 tries, smashing the West, 137-94, at Cincinnati. Cincinnati's Adrian Smith, the last man selected for the game, led the East with 24 points and won MVP honors.

Chamberlain, Lucas, Robertson, Barry, and West made the All-NBA team, with Boston's Bill Russell again back on the second five.

During the season West, Philadelphia's Hal Greer, Baltimore's Bailey Howell, and Boston's Sam Jones all entered the exclusive 10,000-career-point club.

STANDINGS

EASTERN DIVISION

	W.	L.	Pct.
Philadelphia	55	25	.688
Boston	54	26	.675
Cincinnati	45	35	.563
New York	30	50	.375

WESTERN DIVISION

	W.	L.	Pct.
Los Angeles	45	35	.563
Baltimore	38	42	.475
St. Louis	36	44	.450
San Francisco	35	45	.438
Detroit	22	58	.275

PLAYOFFS

FIRST ROUND

Boston defeated Cincinnati 3 games to 2
St. Louis defeated Baltimore 3 games to 0

SEMIFINALS

Boston defeated Philadelphia 4 games to 1
Los Angeles defeated St. Louis 4 games to 3

CHAMPIONSHIP

Boston defeated Los Angeles 4 games to 3

TOP SCORERS

	Pts.	Ave.
Wilt Chamberlain, Philadelphia	2649	33.5
Jerry West, Los Angeles	2476	31.4
Oscar Robertson, Cincinnati	2378	31.3
Rick Barry, San Francisco	2059	25.7
Walt Bellamy, New York	1820	22.8

TOP REBOUNDERS

	No.	Ave.
Wilt Chamberlain, Philadelphia	1943	24.6
Bill Russell, Boston	1779	22.8
Jerry Lucas, Cincinnati	1668	21.8
Nate Thurmond, San Francisco	1312	18.0
Walt Bellamy, New York	1254	15.7

LEADERS IN ASSISTS

	No.	Ave.
Oscar Robertson, Cincinnati	847	11.1
Guy Rodgers, San Francisco	846	10.7
K. C. Jones, Boston	503	6.3
Jerry West, Los Angeles	480	6.1
Howard Komives, New York	426	5.3

MALCOLM EMMONS

Detroit's Dave Bing was top rookie.

Sports' greatest success story ended when the Boston Celtics, NBA champions for the past eight seasons, yielded the league championship to Wilt Chamberlain and the Philadelphia 76ers. The 76ers won the most games (68), had the highest winning percentage (.840) in the history of the league, and finished eight games ahead of the Celtics in the Eastern Division.

Before the season, Red Auerbach, the mastermind of Boston's phenomenal success, had retired and turned the coaching job over to Bill Russell. Russell, who continued as a player, became the first Negro head coach of a major league team in America. Auerbach closed out a 20-year coaching career with a record of 1,037 victories and 548 losses and nine NBA championships.

For the first time since coming into the league, Chamberlain failed to win the scoring title. But under the

154

coaching of Alex Hannum, Chamberlain played the best all-around basketball of his career and excelled on defense and as a playmaker. San Francisco's Rick Barry, in his second pro season, took over as the scoring leader. Barry averaged 35.6 points a game and Chamberlain droppped to third behind Cincinnati's Oscar Robertson. Barry scored 50 or more points six times during the season.

Chamberlain won the Most Valuable Player award for the second straight year and established a record by hitting on 68.3 percent of his field goal attempts. He also led in rebounding with a 24.2 average.

Cincinnati's Adrian Smith led in foul-shooting with a .903 percentage, and Guy Rodgers of Chicago won his second assist title with an average of 11.1 a game.

The NBA returned to Chicago after a three-year absence and the new Chicago Bulls surprised everyone by making the playoffs in their very first season. Much of the credit went to John Kerr, who won Coach of the Year honors. Detroit finished below the Bulls in the West, and Dave DeBusschere, their player-coach, resigned as coach late in the season. He was replaced by Donnis Butcher.

San Francisco, with Barry and Nate Thurmond, won the Western title by five games over the St. Louis Hawks. Philadelphia ousted Boston, four games to one, in the Eastern finals and then downed the Warriors, four games to two, for the NBA championship.

The West, behind Barry, scored a 135-120 triumph in the All-Star Game at San Francisco. Barry scored 40 points on his way to MVP honors.

Barry, Chamberlain, Robertson, and Los Angeles' Elgin Baylor and Jerry West made the All-NBA team and Dave Bing of Detroit was named Rookie of the Year. Bing finished tenth in scoring with a 20.0 average.

New York, after seven years of failure, finally made it into the playoffs. But the Knicks' success was short-lived, as Boston eliminated them, three games to one, in the opening round.

After the season, the NBA, under pressure from the

players, agreed to establish a major medical health insurance program and to institute a pension plan that would pay 10-year veterans of the league $600 a month when they reach age 65.

STANDINGS

EASTERN DIVISION

	W.	L.	Pct.
Philadelphia	68	13	.840
Boston	60	21	.741
Cincinnati	39	42	.481
New York	36	45	.444
Baltimore	20	61	.247

WESTERN DIVISION

	W.	L.	Pct.
San Francisco	44	37	.543
St. Louis	39	42	.481
Los Angeles	36	45	.444
Chicago	33	48	.470
Detroit	30	51	.370

PLAYOFFS

FIRST ROUND

Philadelphia defeated Cincinnati 3 games to 1
Boston defeated New York 3 games to 1
San Francisco defeated Los Angeles 3 games to 0
St. Louis defeated Chicago 3 games to 0

SEMIFINALS

Philadelphia defeated Boston 4 games to 1
San Francisco defeated St. Louis 4 games to 2

CHAMPIONSHIP

Philadelphia defeated San Francisco 4 games
to 2

TOP SCORERS

	Pts.	Ave.
Rick Barry, San Francisco	2775	35.6
Oscar Robertson, Cincinnati	2412	30.5
Wilt Chamberlain, Philadelphia	1956	24.1
Jerry West, Los Angeles	1892	28.7
Elgin Baylor, Los Angeles	1862	26.6

TOP REBOUNDERS

	No.	Ave.
Wilt Chamberlain, Philadelphia	1957	24.2
Bill Russell, Boston	1700	21.0
Jerry Lucas, Cincinnati	1547	19.1
Nate Thurmond, San Francisco	1382	21.3
Bill Bridges, St. Louis	1190	15.1

LEADERS IN ASSISTS

	No.	Ave.
Guy Rodgers, Chicago	908	11.2
Oscar Robertson, Cincinnati	845	10.7
Wilt Chamberlain, Philadelphia	630	7.8
Bill Russell, Boston	472	5.8
Jerry West, Los Angeles	447	6.8

BARTON SILVERMAN

Wilt Chamberlain soars in new Madison Square Garden.

Boston's tired old men battled back to recapture the NBA championship they had held for so long. The Celtics finished second in the East, eight games behind Philadelphia, the defending champion, and then fell behind the 76ers, three games to one, in the Eastern playoff finals.

But with Bill Russell, the 34-year-old player-coach, 35-year-old Sam Jones, 31-year-old Bailey Howell, and John Havlicek, a relative youngster at 28, Boston swept the next three games. The Celtics then went on to crush Los Angeles, four games to two, for their tenth championship in twelve seasons. Los Angeles had finished four games behind St. Louis in the West, but had eliminated the Hawks in four straight games to reach the playoff finals.

Rick Barry, the NBA's leading scorer a year ago, attempted to sign with Oakland of the new American

Basketball Association. Bruce Hale, Barry's father-in-law, was the Oakland coach. But San Francisco brought legal action to stop Barry, and the former Warrior star was forced to sit out the season.

Dave Bing, the Rookie of the Year at Detroit in 1966–67, took over from Barry as the scoring leader. The Pistons' flashy guard averaged 27.1 points a game. Los Angeles' Elgin Baylor, who made an amazing recovery from a knee injury, was second.

Wilt Chamberlain, the NBA's leader in field-goal percentage with a .595 mark, also became the first center ever to lead the league in assists, averaging 8.6 a game. Wilt finished third in the scoring race, but did become the first player to reach a career mark of 25,000 points. Cincinnati's Oscar Robertson led in free-throw accuracy with an .873 percentage and Chamberlain, as usual, was the top rebounder, averaging 23.8 a game.

Bill Bradley, a three-time All-American at Princeton,

Ivy Leaguer and Rhodes scholar Bill Bradley made his debut with the Knicks.

159

finally made his pro debut with the New York Knickerbockers after spending two years at England's Oxford
University as a Rhodes Scholar. Bradley joined the
Knicks in mid-season and averaged only 8.0 points a
game. The Knicks showed tremendous progress, though,
and finished third in the East, their best showing in
10 years. Much of the improvement came after Red
Holzman replaced Dick McGuire as coach in mid-
season.

The NBA added two new franchises, San Diego and
Seattle, to the Western Division, creating a 12-team
league. The San Diego Rockets had the somewhat dubious distinction of losing 67 games, erasing a record
of 63 losses set by San Francisco in 1964–65.

The East scored a 144-124 victory in the All-Star
Game at New York, with Hal Greer of Philadelphia winning the MVP award. Greer tallied 21 points and Havlicek had 26 for the winners.

Chamberlain, the Most Valuable Player for the third
consecutive year, headed the All-NBA team. He was

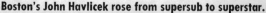

Boston's John Havlicek rose from supersub to superstar.

MALCOLM EMMONS

Baltimore's Earl "The Pearl" Monroe, Rookie of the year, against Royals' Oscar Robertson.

MALCOLM EMMONS

joined by Russell, Bing, Robertson, and Cincinnati's Jerry Lucas. Earl "The Pearl" Monroe, Baltimore's outstanding 6-3 guard, was Rookie of the Year. Monroe averaged 24.3 points a game, fourth in the league, and proved an exciting playmaker and dribbler.

The league announced plans to expand to 14 teams for the 1968–69 season. The owners voted to locate new franchises in Phoenix and Milwaukee. The Phoenix team would be the first major league professional team ever in Arizona.

The NBA owners agreed that beginning with the 1968–69 season, rookies would be paid a minimum of $10,000 a year. This figure would be raised to a minimum of $13,000 for the 1970–71 season. The NBA also agreed to pay veteran players a minimum of $12,500 for 1968–69 and $13,500 the following year. The minimum pay scale was adopted at the urging of the NBA Players Association, whose president was Oscar Robertson.

STANDINGS

EASTERN DIVISION

	W.	L.	Pct.
Philadelphia	62	20	.756
Boston	54	28	.659
New York	43	39	.524
Detroit	40	42	.488
Cincinnati	39	43	.476
Baltimore	36	46	.439

WESTERN DIVISION

	W.	L.	Pct.
St. Louis	56	26	.683
Los Angeles	52	30	.634
San Francisco	43	39	.524
Chicago	29	53	.354
Seattle	23	59	.280
San Diego	15	67	.183

PLAYOFFS

FIRST ROUND

Philadelphia defeated New York 4 games to 2
Boston defeated Detroit 4 games to 2
Los Angeles defeated Chicago 4 games to 1
San Francisco defeated St. Louis 4 games to 2

SEMIFINALS

Boston defeated Philadelphia 4 games to 3
Los Angeles defeated San Francisco 4 games
    to 0

CHAMPIONSHIP

Boston defeated Los Angeles 4 games to 2

TOP SCORERS

	Pts.	Ave.
Dave Bing, Detroit	2142	27.1
Elgin Baylor, Los Angeles	2002	26.0
Wilt Chamberlain, Philadelphia	1992	24.3
Earl Monroe, Baltimore	1991	24.3
Hal Greer, Philadelphia	1976	24.1

TOP REBOUNDERS

	No.	Ave.
Wilt Chamberlain, Philadelphia	1952	23.8
Jerry Lucas, Cincinnati	1560	19.0
Bill Russell, Boston	1451	18.6
Clyde Lee, San Francisco	1141	13.9
Nate Thurmond, San Francisco	1121	22.0

LEADERS IN ASSISTS

	No.	Ave.
Wilt Chamberlain, Philadelphia	702	8.6
Len Wilkens, St. Louis	679	8.3
Oscar Robertson, Cincinnati	633	9.7
Dave Bing, Detroit	509	6.4
Walt Hazzard, Seattle	493	6.2

Player-coach Bill Russell (6) and his Boston Celtics again did in Jerry West and the L.A. Lakers for the title.

UPI

1968-69

163

The Baltimore Bullets, last in the East a year ago, rebounded all the way to first. And the Los Angeles Lakers, adding Wilt Chamberlain to a lineup that already included Elgin Baylor and Jerry West, finished seven games ahead of Atlanta in the West.

But when the playoffs opened, it was the same old story. The Boston Celtics, behind player-coach Bill Russell, had finished fourth in the East, but they eliminated Philadelphia in five games and New York in six to reach the playoff finals. The fast-improving Knicks had previously crushed Baltimore in four straight.

In the Western Division, the star-studded Lakers ousted San Francisco in six games and Atlanta in five, setting up the sixth Boston-Los Angeles playoff final in eight seasons.

As they had so often in the past, the Celtics again emerged victorious for their eleventh NBA title in thirteen seasons, winning a grueling seven-game series that ended with Chamberlain on the bench with a knee injury. Russell paced Boston throughout the playoffs, averaging more than 20 rebounds a game. John Havlicek provided the scoring punch with a 25.4 playoff average. After the season, Russell, the man many regarded as the greatest ever to play in the NBA, and Sam Jones, his long-time Boston teammate, retired.

The season also marked the debuts of two brilliant rookie centers, Wes Unseld of Baltimore and Elvin Hayes of the new San Diego Rockets. Unseld, a steady, unselfish player, proved the key to Baltimore's success and became the first rookie since Chamberlain in 1959–60 to win MVP and Rookie-of-the-Year honors. Hayes won the scoring title with a 28.4 average, comfortably ahead of the Bullets' Earl Monroe. This too, was a title no rookie since Wilt had captured.

Chamberlain won his fifth consecutive field-goal percentage title with a .583 mark and also led the circuit in rebounding with a 21.1 average. Cincinnati's Oscar Robertson took back the assist crown with an average of 9.8 a game and Boston's Larry Siegfried was the league's most accurate foul-shooter, hitting at an .873 clip.

Baylor and Robertson each pushed his career scoring total above 20,000 points, joining Chamberlain and the retired Bob Pettit at that plateau. Boston's Bailey Howell and Sam Jones and Detroit's Walt Bellamy all reached the 15,000-point level.

The East, led by the shooting of Robertson and Monroe, scored a 123-112 triumph in the All-Star Game at Baltimore; Robertson, the game's MVP, scored 24 points and Monroe added 21.

With new franchises in Milwaukee and Phoenix and the St. Louis team shifted to Atlanta, attendance for the 14-team circuit increased 21 percent. A double-header in Houston's Astrodome drew 41,163 spectators, more than doubling the previous attendance record. The NBA also reached another milestone when three playoff games were nationally televised in prime time by the American Broadcasting Company.

Some new faces turned up on the All-NBA team as Unseld, Monroe, and Philadelphia's Billy Cunningham all made the squad for the first time, along with perennial selections Baylor and Robertson. It was a sign of changing times that Russell and Chamberlain, one or the other of whom had been the All-NBA center in every season since 1958–59, both failed to make the team. Gene Shue, the architect of Baltimore's last-to-first recovery, was named Coach of the Year.

STANDINGS

EASTERN DIVISION

	W.	L.	Pct.
Baltimore	57	25	.695
Philadelphia	55	27	.671
New York	54	28	.659
Boston	48	34	.585
Cincinnati	41	41	.500
Detroit	32	50	.390
Milwaukee	27	55	.329

WESTERN DIVISION

	W.	L.	Pct.
Los Angeles	55	27	.671
Atlanta	48	34	.585
San Francisco	41	41	.500
San Diego	37	45	.451
Chicago	33	49	.402
Seattle	30	52	.366
Phoenix	16	66	.195

PLAYOFFS

FIRST ROUND

New York defeated Baltimore 4 games to 0
Boston defeated Philadelphia 4 games to 1
Los Angeles defeated San Francisco 4 games to 2
Atlanta defeated San Diego 4 games to 2

SEMIFINALS

Boston defeated New York 4 games to 2
Los Angeles defeated Atlanta 4 games to 1

FINALS

Boston defeated Los Angeles 4 games to 3

TOP SCORERS

	Pts.	Ave.
Elvin Hayes, San Diego	2327	28.4
Earl Monroe, Baltimore	2065	25.8
Billy Cunningham, Philadelphia	2034	24.8
Bob Rule, Seattle	1965	24.0
Oscar Robertson, Cincinnati	1955	24.7

TOP REBOUNDERS

	No.	Ave.
Wilt Chamberlain, Los Angeles	1712	21.1
Wes Unseld, Baltimore	1491	18.2
Bill Russell, Boston	1484	19.3
Elvin Hayes, San Diego	1406	17.1
Nate Thurmond, San Francisco	1402	19.7

LEADERS IN ASSISTS

	No.	Ave.
Oscar Robertson, Cincinnati	772	9.8
Len Wilkens, Seattle	674	8.2
Walt Frazier, New York	635	7.9
Guy Rodgers, Milwaukee	561	6.9
Dave Bing, Detroit	546	7.1

Knick captain Willis Reed, who became MVP of the playoffs despite injury, gets one off against Milwaukee's Lew Alcindor.

UPI

1969-70

167

The man many felt was destined to be the greatest center ever made his professional debut as the highest-paid rookie in the league's history. But neither Lew Alcindor, the Milwaukee Buck's outstanding million-dollar rookie, nor the Los Angeles Lakers' trio of aging superstars could stop the New York Knickerbockers from winning their first NBA championship.

Combining a well-balanced offense with one of the tightest defenses the league had ever seen, the Knicks topped the Lakers, four games to three, in the playoff finals. This marked the seventh time in nine seasons that Los Angeles lost in the final round of the playoffs. The Knicks, led by Willis Reed, the League's Most Valuable Player, and Walt Frazier, an outstanding playmaker and defender, finished six games ahead of the Bucks in the Eastern Division race, and eliminated the Bucks, four games to one, in the Eastern playoff finals.

But Milwaukee, with the 7-1 Alcindor, a unanimous Rookie-of-the-Year selection, in the middle, loomed as a coming power in the NBA. Last-place finishers with a 27-55 record a year ago, the Bucks improved to a 56-26 mark with the addition of Alcindor. The rookie from UCLA finished second in scoring with a 28.8 average, third in rebounding, and led the league's centers in assists.

In the West, the Atlanta Hawks finished first during the regular season, two games ahead of the Lakers. But Los Angeles was forced to play most of the season without Wilt Chamberlain, who underwent knee surgery early in the campaign. Wilt defied his doctors' predictions, however, by returning for the playoffs, and led the Lakers to a four-game sweep over the Hawks in the Western finals. With Elgin Baylor also injured for much of the season, an additional burden fell on Jerry West, the third of the Laker super-players. West responded admirably, leading the league in scoring with a 31.2 average and finishing second to Reed in the MVP voting.

The final playoff series between New York and Los Angeles featured such highlights as a 60-foot basket by

West that sent the third game into overtime, and a courageous performance by Reed in the seventh game after he suffered a painful muscle injury earlier in the series. In the end, it was the superior balance of the Knicks that carried them to the title in their first appearance in the playoff finals since 1953. Besides Reed and Frazier, the New York starters included Dave DeBusschere, Bill Bradley, and Dick Barnett. Red Holzman, the Coach of the Year, made spectacular use of an explosive bench headed by Cazzie Russell, Mike Riordan, and Dave Stallworth, who returned to action in a phenomenal comeback two years after having suffered a heart attack.

Elvin Hayes of the San Deigo Rockets was the rebounding leader, averaging 16.9 a game. Cincinnati's Johnny Green, a 36-year-old forward, led the league in field-goal accuracy with a .559 percentage, and Len Wilkens, the Seattle player-coach, averaged 9.1 assists a game. Although Wilkens entered the season ranked eighth on the all-time assist list, he had never before led the league in that department. Milwaukee's Flynn Robinson topped the foul shooters with an .898 percentage.

Oscar Robertson, though hampered by injuries, moved into third place among the all-time top scorers, trailing only Chamberlain and Baylor. After the season, Bob Cousy, the first-year coach of the Royals, traded Robertson to Milwaukee for Flynn Robinson and Charlie Paulk, a forward who had spent the last two years in the Army. Earlier in the year Cousy had traded Jerry Lucas, another long-time Cincinnati star, to San Francisco in the first step of a rebuilding program.

The best individual performances of the year included 57 points by Atlanta's Lou Hudson, 37 rebounds by Chicago's Tom Boerwinkle, and 22 assists by San Diego's Art Williams. The Knicks won eighteen consecutive games early in the season, breaking the record of seventeen held by Boston and the old Washington Capitols.

In the annual All-Star Game, played before a capacity crowd in Philadelphia's Spectrum, the East defeated the West, 142-135. Reed, the game's MVP, scored 21 points and Robertson, also with 21, displaced Bob Pettit as the all-time All-Star career scoring leader.

West was the only unanimous choice for the All-NBA team, being selected for the seventh time. He was joined on the squad by the Knicks' Reed and Frazier, Billy Cunningham of Philadelphia, and Connie Hawkins of Phoenix, an exciting newcomer who over the summer had jumped from the rival American Basketball Association. Robertson, a second-team choice, missed first-team honors for the first time since coming into the league in 1960.

The NBA was busy off the court as well, voting to expand to seventeen teams for 1970–71 and battling the ABA for the top college players. The NBA stocked the new Buffalo Braves, Cleveland Cavaliers, and Portland Trail Blazers through an expansion draft that saw such established players as Bailey Howell, Larry Siegfried, LeRoy Ellis and Johnny Egan, and rookie standout Dick Garrett left unprotected.

The league also realigned into four divisions for the 1970–71 season with the following lineup:

Atlantic — New York, Boston, Philadelphia, Buffalo
Central —Atlanta, Baltimore, Cincinnati, Cleveland
Midwest — Chicago, Detroit, Milwaukee, Phoenix
Pacific — Los Angeles, San Francisco, San Diego, Seattle, Portland

In the battle between the leagues, merger seemed imminent. The competition for college stars drove bonuses for several high picks above the million-dollar-mark, and it appeared unlikely that the owners in either the NBA or the ABA could continue spending at that rate. Four NBA referees switched to the ABA, and several outstanding players, including Cunningham, Dave Bing, and Zelmo Beaty, announced they intended to jump to the ABA. The NBA's Detroit franchise signed Bob Lanier and Atlanta signed Pete Maravich, the two chief prizes among the graduating college seniors. But for the first time in its three-year history the ABA signed a significant number of the best college players, including Rick Mount, Charley Scott, Dan Issel and Mike Maloy.

STANDINGS

EASTERN DIVISION

	W.	L.	Pct.
New York	60	22	.732
Milwaukee	56	26	.683
Baltimore	50	32	.610
Philadelphia	42	40	.512
Cincinnati	36	46	.439
Boston	34	48	.415
Detroit	31	51	.378

WESTERN DIVISION

	W.	L.	Pct.
Atlanta	48	34	.585
Los Angeles	46	36	.561
Chicago	39	43	.476
Phoenix	39	43	.476
Seattle	36	46	.439
San Francisco	30	52	.366
San Diego	27	55	.329

PLAYOFFS

FIRST ROUND

Milwaukee defeated Philadelphia 4 games to 1
New York defeated Baltimore 4 games to 3
Atlanta defeated Chicago 4 games to 1
Los Angeles defeated Phoenix 4 games to 3

SEMIFINALS

New York defeated Milwaukee 4 games to 1
Los Angeles defeated Atlanta 4 games to 0

CHAMPIONSHIP

New York defeated Los Angeles 4 games to 3

TOP SCORERS

	Pts.	Ave.
Jerry West, Los Angeles	2309	31.2
Lew Alcindor, Milwaukee	2361	28.8
Elvin Hayes, San Diego	2256	27.5
Billy Cunningham, Philadelphia	2114	26.1
Lou Hudson, Atlanta	2031	25.4

TOP REBOUNDERS

	No.	Ave.
Elvin Hayes, San Diego	1386	16.9
Wes Unseld, Baltimore	1370	16.7
Lew Alcindor, Milwaukee	1190	14.5
Bill Bridges, Atlanta	1181	14.4
Willis Reed, New York	1126	13.9
Gus Johnson, Baltimore	1086	13.9

LEADERS IN ASSISTS

	No.	Ave.
Len Wilkens, Seattle	683	9.1
Walt Frazier, New York	629	8.2
Clem Haskins, Chicago	624	7.6
Jerry West, Los Angeles	554	7.5
Gail Goodrich, Phoenix	605	7.5

1946–47

FIRST	SECOND
Joe Fulks, Philadelphia	Ernie Calverley, Providence
Bob Feerick, Washington	Frank Baumholtz, Cleveland
Stan Miasek, Detroit	John Logan, St. Louis
Bones McKinney, Washington	Chuck Halbert, Chicago
Max Zaslofsky, Chicago	Fred Scolari, Washington

1947–48

Joe Fulks, Philadelphia	John Logan, St. Louis
Max Zaslofsky, Chicago	Carl Braun, New York
Ed Sadowski, Boston	Stan Miasek, Chicago
Howie Dallmar, Philadelphia	Fred Scolari, Washington
Bob Feerick, Washington	Buddy Jeannette, Baltimore

1948–49

George Mikan, Minneapolis	Arnie Risen, Rochester
Joe Fulks, Philadelphia	Bob Feerick, Washington
Bob Davies, Rochester	Bones McKinney, Washington
Max Zaslofsky, Chicago	Ken Sailors, Providence
Jim Pollard, Minneapolis	John Logan, St. Louis

1949–50

George Mikan, Minneapolis	Frank Brian, Anderson
Jim Pollard, Minneapolis	Fred Schaus, Fort Wayne
Alex Groza, Indianapolis	Dolph Schayes, Syracuse
Bob Davies, Rochester	Al Cervi, Syracuse
Max Zaslofsky, Chicago	Ralph Beard, Indianapolis

1950–51

George Mikan, Minneapolis	Dolph Schayes, Syracuse
Alex Groza, Indianapolis	Frank Brian, Tri-Cities
Ed Macauley, Boston	Vern Mikkelsen, Minneapolis
Bob Davies, Rochester	Joe Fulks, Philadelphia
Ralph Beard, Indianapolis	Dick McGuire, New York

1951–52

George Mikan, Minneapolis	Larry Foust, Fort Wayne
Ed Macauley, Boston	Vern Mikkelsen, Minneapolis
Paul Arizin, Philadelphia	Jim Pollard, Minneapolis
Bob Cousy, Boston	Bob Wanzer, Rochester
{ Bob Davies, Rochester { Dolph Schayes, Syracuse	Andy Phillip, Philadelphia

1952–53

George Mikan, Minneapolis	Bill Sharman, Boston
Bob Cousy, Boston	Vern Mikkelsen, Minneapolis
Neil Johnston, Philadelphia	Bob Wanzer, Rochester
Ed Macauley, Boston	Bob Davies, Rochester
Dolph Schayes, Syracuse	Andy Phillip, Philadelphia

ALL-NBA TEAMS

1953–54

FIRST	SECOND
Bob Cousy, Boston	Ed Macauley, Boston
Neil Johnston, Philadelphia	Jim Pollard, Minneapolis
George Mikan, Minneapolis	Carl Braun, New York
Dolph Schayes, Syracuse	Bob Wanzer, Rochester
Harry Gallatin, New York	Paul Seymour, Syracuse

1954–55

Neil Johnston, Philadelphia	Vern Mikkelsen, Minneapolis
Bob Cousy, Boston	Harry Gallatin, New York
Dolph Schayes, Syracuse	Paul Seymour, Syracuse
Bob Pettit, Milwaukee	Slater Martin, Minneapolis
Larry Foust, Fort Wayne	Bill Sharman, Boston

1955–56

Bob Pettit, St. Louis	Dolph Schayes, Syracuse
Paul Arizin, Philadelphia	Maurice Stokes, Rochester
Neil Johnston, Philadelphia	Clyde Lovellette, Minneapolis
Bob Cousy, Boston	Slater Martin, Minneapolis
Bill Sharman, Boston	Jack George, Philadelphia

1956–57

Paul Arizin, Philadelphia	George Yardley, Fort Wayne
Dolph Schayes, Syracuse	Maurice Stokes, Rochester
Bob Pettit, St. Louis	Neil Johnston, Philadelphia
Bob Cousy, Boston	Dick Garmaker, Minneapolis
Bill Sharman, Boston	Slater Martin, St. Louis

1957–58

Dolph Schayes, Syracuse	Cliff Hagan, St. Louis
George Yardley, Detroit	Maurice Stokes, Cincinnati
Bob Pettit, St. Louis	Bill Russell, Boston
Bob Cousy, Boston	Tom Gola, Philadelphia
Bill Sharman, Boston	Slater Martin, St. Louis

1958–59

Bob Pettit, St. Louis	Paul Arizin, Philadelphia
Elgin Baylor, Minneapolis	Cliff Hagan, St. Louis
Bill Russell, Boston	Dolph Schayes, Syracuse
Bob Cousy, Boston	Slater Martin, St. Louis
Bill Sharman, Boston	Richie Guerin, New York

1959–60

Bob Pettit, St. Louis	Jack Twyman, Cincinnati
Elgin Baylor, Minneapolis	Dolph Schayes, Syracuse
Wilt Chamberlain, Philadelphia	Bill Russell, Boston
Bob Cousy, Boston	Richie Guerin, New York
Gene Shue, Detroit	Bill Sharman, Boston

1960–61

FIRST	SECOND
Elgin Baylor, Los Angeles	Tom Heinsohn, Boston
Bob Pettit, St. Louis	Bailey Howell, Detroit
Bill Russell, Boston	Wilt Chamberlain, San Francisco
Oscar Robertson, Cincinnati	Bob Cousy, Boston
Jerry West, Los Angeles	Hal Greer, Syracuse

1961–62

Bob Pettit, St. Louis	Tom Heinsohn, Boston
Elgin Baylor, Los Angeles	Jerry Lucas, Cincinnati
Wilt Chamberlain, San Francisco	Bill Russell, Boston
Oscar Robertson, Cincinnati	John Havlicek, Boston
Jerry West, Los Angeles	Hal Greer, Philadelphia

1962–63

Elgin Baylor, Los Angeles	Bob Pettit, St. Louis
Jerry Lucas, Cincinnati	Gus Johnson, Baltimore
Bill Russell, Boston	Wilt Chamberlain, S. F.-Phila.
Oscar Robertson, Cincinnati	Sam Jones, Boston
Jerry West, Los Angeles	Hal Greer, Philadelphia

1963–64

Rick Barry, San Francisco	John Havlicek, Boston
Jerry Lucas, Cincinnati	Gus Johnson, Boston
Wilt Chamberlain, Philadelphia	Bill Russell, Boston
Oscar Robertson, Cincinnati	Sam Jones, Boston
Jerry West, Los Angeles	Hal Greer, Philadelphia

1964–65

Rick Barry, San Francisco	Willis Reed, New York
Elgin Baylor, Los Angeles	Jerry Lucas, Cincinnati
Wilt Chamberlain, Philadelphia	Bill Russell, Boston
Jerry West, Los Angeles	Hal Greer, Philadelphia
Oscar Robertson, Cincinnati	Sam Jones, Boston

1965–66

Elgin Baylor, Los Angeles	Dolph Schayes, Syracuse
Bob Pettit, St. Louis	Tom Heinsohn, Boston
Wilt Chamberlain, Philadelphia	Bill Russell, Boston
Bob Cousy, Boston	Larry Costello, Syracuse
Oscar Robertson, Cincinnati	Gene Shue, Detroit

1966–67

Bob Pettit, St. Louis	Tom Heinsohn, Boston
Elgin Baylor, Los Angeles	Jack Twyman, Cincinnati
Wilt Chamberlain, Philadelphia	Bill Russell, Boston
Jerry West, Los Angeles	Richie Guerin, New York
Oscar Robertson, Cincinnati	Bob Cousy, Boston

1967–68

FIRST	SECOND
Elgin Baylor, Los Angeles	Willis Reed, New York
Jerry Lucas, Cincinnati	John Havlicek, Boston
Wilt Chamberlain, Philadelphia	Bill Russell, Boston
Dave Bing, Detroit	Hal Greer, Philadelphia
Oscar Robertson, Cincinnati	Jerry West, Los Angeles

1968–69

Billy Cunningham, Philadelphia	John Havlicek, Boston
Elgin Baylor, Los Angeles	Dave DeBusschere, Detroit-New York
Wes Unseld, Baltimore	Willis Reed, New York
Earl Monroe, Baltimore	Hal Greer, Philadelphia
Oscar Robertson, Cincinnati	Jerry West, Los Angeles

1969–70

Billy Cunningham, Philadelphia	John Havlicek, Boston
Connie Hawkins, Phoenix	Gus Johnson, Baltimore
Willis Reed, New York	Lew Alcindor, Milwaukee
Jerry West, Los Angeles	Lou Hudson, Atlanta
Walt Frazier, New York	Oscar Robertson, Cincinnati

ALL-ROOKIE TEAMS

1963–64

Jerry Lucas, Cincinnati
Gus Johnson, Baltimore
Nate Thurmond, San Francisco
Art Heyman, New York
Rod Thorn, Baltimore

1964–65

Willis Reed, New York
Jim Barnes, New York
Howie Komives, New York
Luke Jackson, Philadelphia
Wally Jones, Baltimore
Joe Caldwell, Detroit

1965–66

Rick Barry, San Francisco
Bill Cunningham, Philadelphia
Tom Van Arsdale, Detroit
Dick Van Arsdale, New York
Fred Hetzel, San Francisco

1966–67

Lou Hudson, St. Louis

Jack Marin, Baltimore
Erwin Mueller, Chicago
Cazzie Russell, New York
Dave Bing, Detroit

1967–68

Earl Monroe, Baltimore
Bob Rule, Seattle
Al Tucker, Seattle
Walt Frazier, New York
Phil Jackson, New York

1968–69

Wes Unseld, Baltimore
Elvin Hayes, San Diego
Bill Hewitt, Los Angeles
Art Harris, Seattle
Gary Gregor, Phoenix

1969–70

Lew Alcindor, Milwaukee
Bob Dandridge, Milwaukee
Jo Jo White, Boston
Dick Garrett, Los Angeles
Mike Davis, Baltimore

MOST VALUABLE PLAYER

Podoloff Cup *(By vote of players)*

Year	Player	Team
1955–56	Bob Pettit	St. Louis
1956–57	Bob Cousy	Boston
1957–58	Bill Russell	Boston
1958–59	Bob Pettit	St. Louis
1959–60	Wilt Chamberlain	Philadelphia
1960–61	Bill Russell	Boston
1961–62	Bill Russell	Boston
1962–63	Bill Russell	Boston
1963–64	Oscar Robertson	Cincinnati
1964–65	Bill Russell	Boston
1965–66	Wilt Chamberlain	Philadelphia
1966–67	Wilt Chamberlain	Philadelphia
1967–68	Wilt Chamberlain	Philadelphia
1968–69	Wes Unseld	Baltimore
1969–70	Willis Reed	New York

ROOKIE OF THE YEAR

(By vote of writers)

Year	Player	Team
1952–53	Don Meineke	Fort Wayne
1953–54	Ray Felix	Baltimore
1954–55	Bob Pettit	Milwaukee
1955–56	Maurice Stokes	Rochester
1956–57	Tom Heinsohn	Boston
1957–58	Woody Sauldsberry	Philadelphia
1958–59	Elgin Baylor	Minneapolis
1959–60	Wilt Chamberlain	Philadelphia
1960–61	Oscar Robertson	Cincinnati
1961–62	Walt Bellamy	Chicago
1962–63	Terry Dischinger	Chicago
1963–64	Jerry Lucas	Cincinnati
1964–65	Willis Reed	New York
1965–66	Rick Barry	San Francisco
1966–67	Dave Bing	Detroit
1967–68	Earl Monroe	Baltimore
1968–69	Wes Unseld	Baltimore
1969–70	Lew Alcindor	Milwaukee

III
ALL-TIME NBA RECORDS

INDIVIDUAL
Single Game

Most Points	100	Wilt Chamberlain, Philadelphia, vs N.Y. at Hershey, Pa., Mar. 2, 1962
Most F. G. Attempted	63	Wilt Chamberlain, Philadelphia, vs N.Y. at Hershey, Pa., Mar. 2, 1962
Most F. G. Made	36	Wilt Chamberlain, Philadelphia, vs N.Y. at Hershey, Pa., Mar. 2, 1962
Most F. T. Attempted	34	Wilt Chamberlain, Philadelphia, vs St. Louis at Philadelphia, Feb. 22, 1962
Most F. T. Made	28	Wilt Chamberlain, Philadelphia, vs N.Y. at Hershey, Pa., Mar. 2, 1962
Most Rebounds	55	Wilt Chamberlain, Philadelphia, vs Boston at Philadelphia, Nov. 24, 1960
Most Assists	28	Bob Cousy, Boston, vs Minneapolis at Boston, Feb. 27, 1959
	28	Guy Rodgers, San Francisco, vs St. Louis at San Francisco, Mar. 14, 1963
Most Personal Fouls	8	Don Otten, Tri-Cities, at Sheboygan, Nov. 24, 1949
Most Free Throws Missed	22	Wilt Chamberlain, Philadelphia, vs Seattle, Dec. 1, 1967
Most Consecutive Points	32	Larry Costello, Syracuse, vs Boston at Boston Dec. 8, 1961
Most Consecutive Free Throws	19	Bob Pettit, St. Louis, vs Boston Nov. 22, 1961

179

Season

Most Points	4,029	Wilt Chamberlain, Philadelphia, 1961–62
Highest Average	50.4	Wilt Chamberlain, Philadelphia, 1961–62
Most F. G. Attempted	3,159	Wilt Chamberlain, Philadelphia, 1961–62
Most F. G. Made	1,597	Wilt Chamberlain, Philadelphia, 1961–62
Highest F. G. Percentage	.683	Wilt Chamberlain, Philadelphia, 1966–67
Most F. T. Attempted	1,363	Wilt Chamberlain, Philadelphia, 1961–62
Most F. T. Made	840	Jerry West, Los Angeles, 1965–66
Highest F. T. Percentage	.932	Bill Sharman, Boston, 1958–59
Most Rebounds	2,149	Wilt Chamberlain, Philadelphia, 1960–61
Most Assists	908	Guy Rodgers, Chicago, 1966–67
Most Personal Fouls	366	Bill Bridges, St. Louis, 1967–68
Most Disqualifications	26	Don Meineke, Fort Wayne, 1952–53

Career

Most Points Scored	27,426	Wilt Chamberlain, Philadelphia Warriors, San Francisco Warriors, Philadelphia 76ers, Los Angeles, 1959–70
Highest Scoring Average	34.3	Wilt Chamberlain, 1959–70
Most F. G. Attempted	20,943	Wilt Chamberlain, 1959–70
Most F. G. Made	11,091	Wilt Chamberlain, 1959–70
Highest F. G. Percentage	.529	Wilt Chamberlain, 1959–70
Most F. T. Attempted	10,210	Wilt Chamberlain, 1959–70
Most F. T. Made	6,979	Dolph Schayes, Syracuse, Philadelphia 76ers, 1948–64

Highest F. T. Percentage	.883	Bill Sharman, Washington, Boston, 1950–61
Most Rebounds	21,721	Bill Russell, Boston, 1956–69
Most Assists	7,731	Oscar Robertson, Cincinnati, 1960–70
Most Minutes Played	40,726	Bill Russell, 1956–69
Most Personal Fouls	3,667	Dolph Schayes, 1948–64
Most Times Disqualified	127	Vern Mikkelsen, Minnesota, 1949–59
Most Games Played	1,059	Dolph Schayes, Syracuse, Philadelphia 76ers, 1948–64

TEAM RECORDS

Single Game

Most Points, One Team	173	Boston vs Minneapolis at Boston, Feb. 27, 1959
Most Points, Two Teams	316	Philadelphia 169, New York 147 at Hershey, Pa., Mar. 2, 1962
	316	Cincinnati 165, San Diego 151 at Cincinnati, Mar. 12, 1970
Most F. G. Attempted, One Team	153	Philadelphia vs Los Angeles at Philadelphia, Dec. 8, 1961
Most F.G. Attempted, Two Teams	291	Philadelphia 153, Los Angeles 138 at Philadelphia, Dec. 8, 1961
Most F.G. Made, One Team	72	Boston vs Minneapolis at Boston, Feb. 27, 1959
Most F.G. Made, Two Teams	134	Cincinnati 67, San Diego 67 at Cincinnati, Mar. 12, 1970
Most F. T. Attempted, One Team	86	Syracuse vs Anderson at Syracuse (In 5 overtimes), Nov. 24, 1949

Most F. T. Attempted, Two Teams	160	Syracuse 86, Anderson 74 at Syracuse (In 5 overtimes), Nov. 24, 1949
Most F. T. Made, One Team	59	Syracuse vs Anderson at Syracuse (In 5 overtimes), Nov. 24, 1949
Most F. T. Made, Two Teams	116	Syracuse 59, Anderson 57 at Syracuse (In 5 overtimes), Nov. 24, 1949
Most Rebounds, One Team	112	Philadelphia vs Cincinnati at Philadelphia Nov. 8, 1959
	112	Boston vs Detroit at Boston, Dec. 24, 1960
Most Rebounds, Two Teams	215	Philadelphia 110, Los Angeles 105 at Philadelphia (In 3 overtimes), Dec. 8, 1961
Most Assists, One Team	60	Boston at Baltimore (In 1 overtime) Nov. 15, 1952
Most Assists, Two Teams	88	Phoenix 47, San Diego 41, Mar. 15, 1969
Most Personal Fouls, One Team	66	Anderson at Syracuse (In 5 overtimes), Nov. 24, 1949
Most Personal Fouls, Two Teams	122	Anderson 66, Syracuse 56 at Syracuse (In 5 overtimes), Nov. 24, 1949
Most Disqualifications, One Team	8	Syracuse vs Baltimore at Syracuse (In 1 overtime), Nov 15, 1952
Most Disqualifications, Two Teams	13	Syracuse 8, Baltimore 5 at Syracuse (In 1 overtime), Nov. 15, 1952
Most Points in a Losing Game	151	San Diego vs Cincinnati at Cincinnati, Mar. 12, 1970

Widest Point Spread	62	Syracuse 162, New York 100, Dec. 25, 1960
Most Consecutive Points in a Game	24	Philadelphia vs Baltimore, Mar. 20, 1966

Season

Most Games Won	68	Philadelphia, 1966–67
Most Games Lost	67	San Diego, 1967–68
Longest Winning Streak	18	New York, Oct. 24, 1969 to Nov. 28, 1969
Longest Losing Streak	17	San Francisco, Dec. 20, 1964 to Jan. 26, 1965
	17	San Diego, Jan. 17, 1968 to Feb. 18, 1968
Most Points Scored	10,143	Philadelphia, 1966–67
Most Points Allowed	10,261	Seattle, 1967–68
Highest Scoring Average	125.4	Philadelphia, 1961–62
Highest Average, Points Allowed	125.1	Seattle, 1967–68
Most F. G. Attempted	9,295	Boston, 1960–61
Most F. G. Made	3,965	Philadelphia, 1967–68
Highest F. G. Percentage	.488	Milwaukee, 1969–70
Most F. T. Attempted	3,411	Phoenix, 1969–70
Most F. T. Made	2,434	Detroit, 1960–61
Highest F. T. Percentage	.794	Syracuse, 1956–57
Most Rebounds	6,131	Boston, 1960–61
Most Assists	2,214	Seattle, 1969–70

ALL-TIME CLUB RECORDS

Season	Coach	W.	L.
	ANDERSON PACKERS		
1949–50	Howard Schultz (21–14)		
	Ike Duffey (1–2)		
	Doxie Moore (15–11)	37	27
	Totals	37	27

Season	Coach	W.	L.
	ATLANTA HAWKS		
1949–50	Roger Potter (1–6)		
	Arnold Auerbach (28–29)	29	35
1950–51	Dave McMillan (9–14)		
	John Logan (2–1)		
	Marko Todorovich (14–28)	25	43
1951–52*	Doxie Moore	17	49
1952–53	Andrew Levane	27	44
1953–54	Andrew Levane (11–35)		
	William Holzman (10–16)	21	51
1954–55	William Holzman	26	46
1955–56**	William Holzman	33	39
1956–57	William Holzman (14–19)		
	Slater Martin (5–3)		
	Alex Hannum (15–16)	34	38
1957–58	Alex Hannum	41	31
1958–59	Andy Phillip (6–4)		
	Ed Macauley (43–19)	49	23
1959–60	Ed Macauley	46	29
1960–61	Paul Seymour	51	28
1961–62	Paul Seymour (5–9)		
	Andrew Levane (20–40)		
	Bob Pettit (4–2)	29	51
1962–63	Harry Gallatin	48	32
1963–64	Harry Gallatin	46	34
1964–65	Harry Gallatin (17–16)		
	Richie Guerin (28–19)	45	35
1965–66	Richie Guerin	36	44
1966–67	Richie Guerin	39	42
1967–68***	Richie Guerin	56	26
1968–69	Richie Guerin	48	34
1969–70	Richie Guerin	48	34
	Totals	794	788

*Team moved from Tri-Cities to Milwaukee
**Team moved from Milwaukee to St. Louis
***Team moved from St. Louis to Atlanta at end of season

Season	Coach	W.	L.
	BALTIMORE BULLETS		
1947–48	Buddy Jeannette	28	20
1948–49	Buddy Jeannette	29	31
1949–50	Buddy Jeannette	25	43
1950–51	Buddy Jeannette (14–23)		
	Walt Budko (10–19)	24	42
1951–52	Fred Scolari (12–27)		
	John Reiser (8–19)	20	46
1952–53	John Reiser (0–3)		
	Clair Bee (16–51)	16	54
1953–54	Clair Bee	16	56
1954–55*	Clair Bee (2–9)		
	Al Barthelme (1–2)	3	11
	Totals	161	303

*Team disbanded Nov. 27, 1954

Season	Coach	W.	L.
	BALTIMORE BULLETS		
1961–62*	Jim Pollard	18	62
1962–63**	Jack McMahon (12–26)		
	Bob Leonard (13–29)	25	55
1963–64***	Bob Leonard	31	49
1964–65	Buddy Jeannette	37	43
1965–66	Paul Seymour	38	42
1966–67	Mike Farmer (1–8)		
	Buddy Jeanette (3–13)		
	Gene Shue (16–40)	20	61
1967–68	Gene Shue	36	46
1968–69	Gene Shue	57	25
1969–70	Gene Shue	50	32
	Totals	312	415

*Played in Chicago as Chicago Packers
**Played in Chicago as Chicago Zephyrs
***Moved to Baltimore, changed name to Bullets

Season	Coach	W.	L.
	BOSTON CELTICS		
1946–47	John Russell	22	38
1947–48	John Russell	20	28
1948–49	Alvin Julian	25	35
1949–50	Alvin Julian	22	46
1950–51	Arnold Auerbach	39	30
1951–52	Arnold Auerbach	39	27
1952–53	Arnold Auerbach	46	25

Season	Coach	W.	L.
1953–54	Arnold Auerbach	42	30
1954–55	Arnold Auerbach	36	36
1955–56	Arnold Auerbach	39	33
1956–57	Arnold Auerbach	44	28
1957–58	Arnold Auerbach	49	23
1958–59	Arnold Auerbach	52	20
1959–60	Arnold Auerbach	59	16
1960–61	Arnold Auerbach	57	22
1961–62	Arnold Auerbach	60	20
1962–63	Arnold Auerbach	58	22
1963–64	Arnold Auerbach	59	21
1964–65	Arnold Auerbach	62	18
1965–66	Arnold Auerbach	54	26
1966–67	Bill Russell	60	21
1967–68	Bill Russell	54	28
1968–69	Bill Russell	48	34
1969–70	Tom Heinsohn	31	51
	Totals	1077	678

Season	Coach	W.	L.
	CHICAGO BULLS		
1966–67	John Kerr	33	48
1967–68	John Kerr	29	53
1968–69	Dick Motta	33	49
1969–70	Dick Motta	39	43
	Totals	134	193

CHICAGO PACKERS

See Baltimore Bullets, 1961–62

Season	Coach	W.	L.
	CHICAGO STAGS		
1946–47	Harold Olsen	39	22
1947–48	Harold Olsen	28	20
1948–49	Harold Olsen (28–21)		
	Philip Brownstein (10–1)	38	22
1949–50	Philip Brownstein	40	28
	Totals	145	92

CHICAGO ZEPHYRS

See Baltimore Bullets, 1962–63

Season	Coach	W.	L.
	CINCINNATI ROYALS		
1948–49	Les Harrison	45	15
1949–50	Les Harrison	51	17
1950–51	Les Harrison	41	27
1951–52	Les Harrison	41	25
1952–53	Les Harrison	44	26
1953–54	Les Harrison	44	28
1954–55	Les Harrison	29	43
1955–56	Bob Wanzer	31	41
1956–57	Bob Wanzer	31	41
1957–58*	Bob Wanzer	33	39
1958–59	Bob Wanzer (3–15)		
	Tom Marshall (16–38)	19	53
1959–60	Tom Marshall	19	56
1960–61	Charles Wolf	33	46
1961–62	Charles Wolf	43	37
1962–63	Charles Wolf	42	38
1963–64	Jack McMahon	55	25
1964–65	Jack McMahon	48	32
1965–66	Jack McMahon	45	35
1966–67	Jack McMahon	39	42
1967–68	Ed Jucker	39	43
1968–69	Ed Jucker	41	41
1969–70	Bob Cousy	36	46
	Totals	849	796

Team moved from Rochester to Cincinnati

Season	Coach	W.	L.
	CLEVELAND REBELS		
1946–47	Dutch Dehnert (17–20)		
	Roy Clifford (13–10)	30	30
	Totals	30	30
	DENVER NUGGETS		
1949–50	James Darden	11	51
	DETROIT FALCONS		
1946–47	Glenn Curtis (12–22)		
	Philip Sachs (8–18)	20	40
	Totals	20	40
	DETROIT PISTONS		
1948–49	Carl Bennett (0–6)		
	Paul Armstrong (22–32)	22	38
1949–50	Murray Mendenhall	40	28

1950–51	Murray Mendenhall	32	36
1951–52	Paul Birch	29	37
1952–53	Paul Birch	36	33
1953–54	Paul Birch	40	32
1954–55	Charles Eckman	43	29
1955–56	Charles Eckman	37	35
1956–57	Charles Eckman	34	38
1957–58*	Charles Eckman (9–16)		
	Ephraim Rocha (24–23)	33	39
1958–59	Ephraim Rocha	28	44
1959–60	Ephraim Rocha (13–21)		
	Dick McGuire (17–24)	30	45
1960–61	Dick McGuire	34	45
1961–62	Dick McGuire	37	43

*Team moved from Fort Wayne to Detroit

Season	Coach	W.	L.
1962–63	Dick McGuire	34	46
1963–64	Charles Wolf	23	57
1964–65	Charles Wolf (2–9)		
	Dave DeBusschere (29–40)	31	49
1965–66	Dave DeBusschere	22	58
1966–67	Dave DeBusschere (28–45)		
	Donnis Butcher (2–6)	30	51
1967–68	Donnis Butcher	40	42
1968–69	Donnis Butcher (10–12)		
	Paul Seymour (22–38)	32	50
1969–70	Bill van Breda Kolff	31	51
	Totals	**718**	**926**

FORT WAYNE PISTONS

See Detroit Pistons, 1957–58

INDIANAPOLIS JETS

1948–49	Bruce Hale (4–13)		
	Burl Friddle (14–29)	18	42

INDIANAPOLIS OLYMPIANS

1949–50	Clifford Barker	39	25
1950–51	Clifford Barker (24–32)		
	Wallace Jones (7–5)	31	37
1951–52	Herman Schaefer	34	32
1952–53	Herman Schaefer	28	43
	Totals	**132**	**137**

LOS ANGELES LAKERS

1948–49	John Kundla	44	16
1949–50	John Kundla	51	17
1950–51	John Kundla	44	24

1951–52	John Kundla	46	26
1952–53	John Kundla	48	22
1953–54	John Kundla	40	26
1954–55	John Kundla	40	32
1955–56	John Kundla	33	39
1956–57	John Kundla	34	38
1957–58	George Mikan (9–30)		
	John Kundla (10–23)	19	53
1958–59	John Kundla	33	39
1959–60	John Castellani (11–25)		
	Jim Pollard (14–25)	25	50
1960–61*	Fred Schaus	36	43
1961–62	Fred Schaus	54	26
1962–63	Fred Schaus	53	27
1963–64	Fred Schaus	42	38
1964–65	Fred Schaus	49	31
1965–66	Fred Schaus	45	35
1966–67	Fred Schaus	36	45
1967–68	Bill van Breda Kolff	52	30
1968–69	Bill van Breda Kolff	55	27
1969–70	Joe Mullaney	46	36
	Totals	925	710

Team moved from Minneapolis to Los Angeles

MILWAUKEE HAWKS
See Atlanta Hawks, 1951–52

MILWAUKEE BUCKS

1968–99	Larry Costello	27	55
1969–70	Larry Costello	56	26
	Totals	83	81

MINNEAPOLIS LAKERS
See Los Angeles Lakers, 1960–61

Season	Coach	W.	L.

NEW YORK KNICKERBOCKERS

1946–47	Neil Cohalan	33	27
1947–48	Joe Lapchick	26	22
1948–49	Joe Lapchick	32	28
1949–50	Joe Lapchick	40	28
1950–51	Joe Lapchick	36	30
1951–52	Joe Lapchick	37	29
1952–53	Joe Lapchick	47	23
1953–54	Joe Lapchick	44	28
1954–55	Joe Lapchick	34	38
1955–56	Joe Lapchick (26–25)		
	Vince Boryla (9–12)	35	37

189

Season	Coach	W.	L.
PHOENIX SUNS			
1968–69	John Kerr	16	66
1969–70	John Kerr (15–23)		
	Jerry Colangelo (24–20)	39	43
	Totals	55	109
PITTSBURGH IRONMEN			
1946–47	Paul Birch	15	45
PROVIDENCE STEAMROLLERS			
1946–47	Robert Morris	28	32
1947–48	Albert Soar (2–17)		
	Nat Hickey	6	42
1948–49	Ken Loeffler	12	48
	Totals	46	122
ST. LOUIS BOMBERS			
1946–47	Ken Loeffler	38	33
1947–48	Ken Loeffler	29	19
1948–49	Grady Lewis	29	31
1949–50	Grady Lewis	26	42
	Totals	122	125
ST. LOUIS HAWKS			
	See Atlanta Hawks, 1967–68		
SAN DIEGO ROCKETS			
1967–68	Jack McMahon	15	67
1968–69	Jack McMahon	37	45
1969–70	Jack McMahon (9–17)		
	Alex Hannum (18–38)	27	55
	Totals	79	167
SAN FRANCISCO WARRIORS			
1946–47	Edward Gottlieb	35	25
1947–48	Edward Gottlieb	27	21
1948–49	Edward Gottlieb	28	32
1949–50	Edward Gottlieb	26	42
1950–51	Edward Gottlieb	40	26
1951–52	Edward Gottlieb	33	33
1952–53	Edward Gottlieb	12	57
1953–54	Edward Gottlieb	29	43
1954–55	Edward Gottlieb	33	39
1955–56	George Senesky	45	27
1956–57	George Senesky	37	35
1957–58	George Senesky	37	35
1958–59	Al Cervi	32	40

1956–57	Vince Boryla	36	36
1957–58	Vince Boryla	35	37
1958–59	Andrew Levane	40	32
1959–60	Andrew Levane (8–19)		
	Carl Braun (19–29)	27	48
1960–61	Carl Braun	21	58
1961–62	Eddie Donovan	29	51
1962–63	Eddie Donovan	21	59
1963–64	Eddie Donovan	22	58
1964–65	Eddie Donovan (12–26)		
	Harry Gallatin (19–23)	31	49
1965–66	Harry Gallatin (6–15)		
	Dick McGuire (24–35)	30	50
1966–67	Dick McGuire	36	45
1967–68	Dick McGuire (15–22)		
	Wiliam Holzman (28–17)	43	39
1968–69	William Holzman	54	28
1969–70	William Holzman	60	22
	Totals	853	898

PHILADELPHIA WARRIORS

See San Francisco Warriors, 1962–63

PHILADELPHIA 76ERS

1949–50	Al Cervi	51	13
1950–51	Al Cervi	32	34
1951–52	Al Cervi	40	26
1952–53	Al Cervi	47	24
1953–54	Al Cervi	42	30
1954–55	Al Cervi	43	29
1955–56	Al Cervi	35	37
1956–57	Al Cervi (4–8)		
	Paul Seymour (34–26)	38	34
1957–58	Paul Seymour	41	31
1958–59	Paul Seymour	35	37
1959–60	Paul Seymour	45	30
1960–61	Alex Hannum	38	41
1961–62	Alex Hannum	41	39
1962–63	Alex Hannum	48	32
1963–64*	Dolph Schayes	34	46
1964–65	Dolph Schayes	40	40
1965–66	Dolph Schayes	55	25
1966–67	Alex Hannum	68	13
1967–68	Alex Hannum	62	20
1968–69	Jack Ramsay	55	27
1969–70	Jack Ramsay	42	40
	Totals	932	648

*Team moved from Syracuse to Philadelphia, changed name to 76ers

191

1959–60	Neil Johnston	49	26
1960–61	Neil Johnston	46	33
1961–62	Frank McGuire	49	31
1962–63*	Bob Feerick	31	49
1963–64	Alex Hannum	48	32
1964–65	Alex Hannum	17	63
1965–66	Alex Hannum	35	45
1966–67	Bill Sharman	44	37
1967–68	Bill Sharman	43	39
1968–69	George Lee	41	41
1969–70	George Lee (22–30)		
	Al Attles (8–22)	30	52
	Totals	847	903

*Team moved from Philadelphia to San Francisco

SEATTLE SUPERSONICS

1967–68	Al Bianchi	23	59
1968–69	Al Bianchi	30	52
1969–70	Len Wilkens	36	46
	Totals	89	157

SHEBOYGAN REDSKINS

1949–50	Ken Suesens	22	40

SYRACUSE NATIONALS

See Philadelphia 76ers, 1963–64

TORONTO HUSKIES

1946–47	Ed Sadowski (3–9)		
	Lew Hayman (0–1)		
	Dick Fitzgerald (2–1)		
	Robert Rolfe (17–27)	22	38

TRI-CITIES BLACKHAWKS

See Atlanta Hawks, 1951–52

WASHINGTON CAPITOLS

1946–47	Arnold Auerbach	49	11
1947–48	Arnold Auerbach	28	20
1948–49	Arnold Auerbach	38	22
1949–50	Bob Feerick	32	36
1950–51*	Horace McKinney	10	25
	Totals	157	114

*Team disbanded January 9, 1951

WATERLOO HAWKS

1949–50	Charles Shipp (8–27)		
	Jack Smile (11–16)	19	43